JEET KUNE DO

Hardcore Training & Strategies Guide

By Larry Hartsell

A HnL PUBLICATION

JEET KUNE DO

HARDCORE TRAINING & STRATEGIES GUIDE

BY LARRY HARTSELL

INTRODUCTION BY PAULA INOSANTO

Featuring:
Dan Inosanto
Justin Williams

Photography by: Eric Heath (Santa Monica, Los Angeles)
Photographs shot at: Inosanto Academy – Los Angeles

Publisher: F.M. Rafiq
International Standard Book No: 09531766-6-5

Published by: HNL Publishing
Email address: hnlpubinquiry@hotmail.com

Disclaimer: Neither the author nor the publisher assumes any responsibility in any manner whatsoever for any injury which may occur by reading, following the instructions herein. Consult your physician before following any of the activities.

DEDICATION

To Debra, my wife, and loving partner.

ACKNOWLEDGMENTS

To my Sifu Guru Dan Inosanto, my mentor and personal friend
for over forty years.
To Simo Paula Inosanto for writing the book's Foreward/Introduction and for support and
friendship over the many years.

Special thanks to the Inosanto Academy of Martial Arts for their assistance and use of the
Academy to shoot the photographs and demonstrations.

To Fred Brown for his knowledge in the Arts and his assistance with this book.

Guro Dan, Simo Paula and Daniel Inosanto

Inosanto Academy of Martial Arts

I want to thank everyone who assisted me in multiple roles in making this possible.

Guro Dan Inosanto, Simo Paula Inosanto, Simo Debra Hartsell, Fred Brown, Erik Paulson,
Judo Gene Labell, Justin Williams, Inosanto Academy of Martial Arts staff and those
featured in my book. Our photographer Eric Heath and his wife (N. Eric Heath
Photography)

To my family, Dale and Joyce Hartsell, Jack and Linda Crosier, Wayne and Tammy Melton
for their constant love, support and strength.

To my students worldwide for their loyalty and continued support in the Arts

TABLE OF CONTENTS

PUBLISHER'S PREFACE

Attempting to encapsulate fighting – which is evidently physical and dynamic – into words and pictures is no easy task. It is even much more difficult to condense into one single tome of the magnitude of elements what encompass Bruce Lee's art and philosophy – which is relatively much more intricate – of Jeet Kune Do.

Larry Hartsell, Bruce Lee's original student and one of the world's leading Jeet Kune Do authorities will inject you with a massive dose of enthusiasm leaving you fortified and making you profoundly omniscient in the art of Jeet Kune Do. Hartsell is a best selling author and an respected authority on an international basis.

In this professionally produced book – fully illustrated combined with a treasure trove of data – Hartsell for the first time culminates many intermediate and advanced levels of Bruce Lees Jeet Kune Do. To your delight you will discover a plethora of training drills and techniques, tactics and fighting strategies, the quantity and calibre of the material guarantees to elevate you to your highest level.

Although an individual may study a martial art for diverse reasons – whether its for self – improvement, self-cultivation, discipline, sport or self defence – the fact remains that it is a physical endeavour. Superficially, the martial arts are seen as essentially physical in nature, primarily concerned with elements as physical conditioning, skill, fitness, technique and tactics. Nothing could be further from the truth.

When we pursue something so passionately, its rewards become tangible, and we pursue to acquire as much information as possible. Any scientist will tell you that research is never an end, rather it is merely a beginning. One may think he knows it all but will soon discover there's always a need for improvement. Books are an invaluable source for accumulating knowledge and gathering essential data.

Here is your road map to an exciting and illuminating journey to achieving excellence in Bruce Lee's Jeet Kune Do and martial arts – a goldmine of information dispensed first hand by Bruce Lees original disciple Larry Hartsell.

I am honoured to have been asked to write this foreward for Larry Hartsell's new book.

You, no doubt are probably wondering why Larry would have asked me, instead of one of the many well known, world renowned martial artists Larry knows and has worked with throughout his 40+ years in the arts. I wondered the same thing. Larry and his wife Debra gave me a very simply answer to this question: "Because you know Larry, probably b etter than anyone, except for your husband". My husband is Dan Inosanto.

Dan and Larry have been best friends, more like brothers for over 40 years. I have known Larry for nearly 20 years, but through my husband's stories, journals and diaries I feel I also knew Larry for those additional 20 years, that date back to their days together with Mr Ed Parker, continuing through their years with the late Bruce Lee, and most significantly life after the tragic passing of Bruce.

Many individuals would have been content to have their fame and notoriety based solely on the fact that "they were original students" of Bruce Lee and Dan Inosanto during the days of the Jun Fan Institute in Los Angeles' Chinatown". Not Larry. Having been an accomplished martial artist, competitor and fighter before he became a studednt in Chinatown. Larry always knew the benefit of 'cross training' and what would really work if one's skills were put to the test in the 'real world', outside the confines of the martial arts dojo or training hall.

Constantly training and honing his skills, so that his students will have that 'edge' that is needed more today than ever before in the martial arts, Larry has put together this book to help students perfect that edge, utilizing techniques, principles and stragegies that while developed in the '60s by Bruce Lee, can still be effective if used today.

The Martial Arts arena of today is far different than it was 40 years ago. If you take the time to explore, along with Larry, the best of the past and utilize it with the knowledge, skill and training of the present, you will not be disappointed. If you have the opportunity to train with Larry, all the better to feel the techniques come to life.
No matter what your level in the Arts, novice or time-worn veteran, you will be able to step into the stil fascinating world, the art and philisophy of Jeet Kune Do with your guide, Mr Larry Hartsell.

Paula L. Inosanto

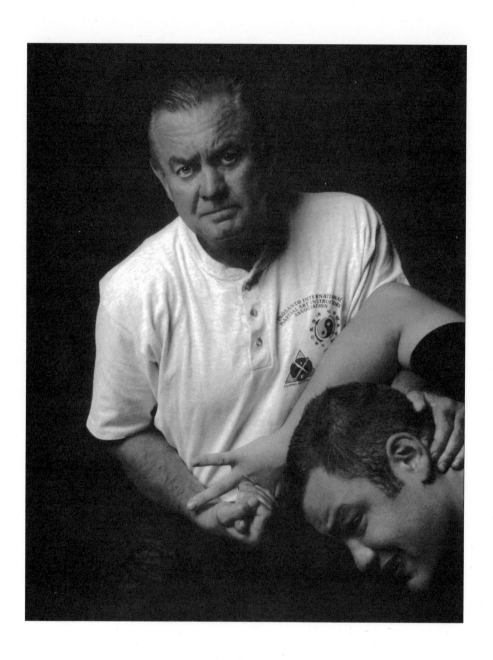

BIOGRAPHY

Larry Hartsell started his martial arts training in 1957 when he enrolled in a judo club in his home town of Charlotte, North Carolina, which he continued up till 1960. He also wrestled in high school further taking part in contact sport and experience grappling. In 1960 he moved to Los Angeles, California, where he began studying Kenpo Karate in 1961under the late great Ed Parker. After receiving his black belt in Kenpo Karate, he was inducted into the army and went on to serve his country in Vietnam from 1966 to 1967, where he served as a military policeman.

After his discharge from the armed forces in 1967, Larry was fortunate to become a member of Bruce Lees private Los Angeles Chinatown school located on 628 college street – Jun Fan Gung Fu Institute. This was a closed door school which one could not just walk in, one had to be invited personally. In addition to training at the Chinatown school, Larry was a member of an elite select few original students that personally trained with Bruce Lee at his house. Apart from sharing a student – instructor relationship with Bruce Lee, Larry was fortunate to have been a good friend who enjoyed talking about martial arts and hanging out together. After the untimely death of his instructor and friend Bruce Lee, Larry continued to constantly immerse himself to reach his full potential as a martial artist, and to this day he has been a close family friend of the Lee family.

In 1973, Larry moved back to his native North Carolina and opened up the only authorised Jeet Kune Do school east of California, where he began teaching carefully screened students Jeet Kune Do. In addition to the Inosanto Academy and the Kali Academy (both based in Los Angeles) this was the only other authorised place for learning Jeet Kune Do in the world.

Larry Hartsell in his personal home garage gym

In 1982 Larry moved back to Los Angeles where he started teaching his own JKD class at the old Inosanto Academy. He began working as a professional bodyguard (Cliff Stewart a student of Larry's and the most sought after bodyguard in history got him involved into professional bodyguarding) to Hollywood celebrities and the rich and famous, including Mr T of THE A TEAM fame, Larry Flint of Hustler magazine and various Saudi sheiks in Beverly Hills. Larry along with Dan Inosanto and Dr Bob Ward have been the conditioning coaches to professional football teams Dallas Cowboys and San Francisco 49ers.

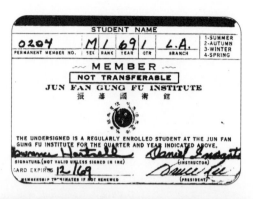

Larry Hartsell's original membership card for Bruce Lee's private school

Dubbed as the 'premier JKD streetfighter' Larry has worked as a professional bouncer in biker bars in North Carolina where he has had to use his practical skills against the rough and tough. Larry is the only original student of Bruce Lee from the LA Chinatown school to have fought a full contact fight for Lee which evidently became the first ever full contact kickboxing fight. Larry's vast experience in hand to hand combat and ten years of practical experience in law enforcement including his service as a deputy sheriff, lead him to teach law enforcement officers and agencies self defense and baton tactics. He also has associate degree in criminology.

At the time of Bruce Lee's untimely death there were limited formal techniques in the Jeet Kune Do grappling range. Larry has continued his pursuit of investigating and integrating concepts into his original Jeet Kune Do framework as taught to him by Bruce Lee to strengthen the grappling range, thus making it much more effective.

Hartsell has appeared on magazine covers worldwide from Inside Kung fu, Black belt, Karate Kung fu Illustrated, Impact, combat, and Australasian Fighting Arts. He has also produced a series of instructional videos that focus on a diverse aspects of training and fighting. He's a best-selling Jeet Kune Do author having authored a total of four classic Jeet Kune Do books including the acclaimed 'Jeet Kune Do conditioning and grappling methods'.

Jun Fan Jeet Kune Do Grappling Association founded by Larry Hartsell ten years ago was formed to propagate and promote training and fighting aspects of Bruce Lees Jeet

Larry Hartsell with Bruce Lee's original Makiwara pad

Kune Do with the prime emphasis put on the grappling component of the art. Today Hartsell who is an internationally recognised senior Jeet Kune Do instructor and personalty continues to give seminars world wide. In addition he teaches at his home in Los Angeles out of his garage handful of students on a one-on-one personal basis only. Dan Inosanto, Larry's mentor and close friend spend as much time as possible in pursuit of continuing their research in their quest for 'truth' in combat. He is one of a few individuals to have been certified as a senior full instructor in Jeet Kune Do.

Many consider Hartsell to be one of the most knowledgeable and world renowned Jeet Kune Do grappling authorities, and a prime force behind the promotion and perpetuation of Bruce Lees art on a worldwide level. With over 40 years of learning, coaching and practical experience Larry Hartsell is truly an American icon and grapplers, as well as the leading forces behind the propagation of Bruce Lees Jeet Kune Do for the past three decades. He is the hard man of JKD.

Larry Hartsell working out in his garage home gym

Bruce Lee, Larry Hartsell and Dan Inosanto

BRUCE LEE – FOUNDER OF JKD

Idolized by millions, what is so intriguing about Bruce Lee that inspired –and – continues to inspire – millions from all walks of life. What is it that made Bruce Lee one of the most unique, rare, and fascinating public figures of the 20th century. Apart from his extraordinary physical attributes and never before seen state of the art fight choreography, Bruce Lee had a composite of facets and critical ingredients which he was able to amalgamate that eventually culminated his personality.

Bruce Lee, no doubt was the greatest martial arts exponent of the century. Idolized by millions all over the world, remarkably this legend has stood the test of time who's achievements and abilities have never been surpassed. Extraordinarily, in a space of only a few short years, Bruce Lee had an enormous impact on millions of people all around the globe. So what exactly set him apart – and continues to do so – from his peers and other public figures and celebrities.

It is important to promulgate that Lee was far from just a martial artist whose extraordinary skills, innovations and insights revolutionised the martial art world – and an exciting movie star who single handedly gave the gift of kung fu to the world unstintingly.

These are just two facets to this most intriguing man. Apart from the premier martial artist of the century and an international movie star, Bruce Lee was a dedicated and astute philosopher who cultivated a personal philosophy that continues to enrich and inspire people from all walks of life. He was a fortifying and edifying teacher who's philosophical teachings and insights encouraged martial artists to explore themselves and dig deeper to come to understand themselves and combat. Last but not least, Lee was a fitness afficiando and a paragon of health and fitness (Athlete) who pushed himself beyond the limits in his quest for physical perfection and cultivation through intense training and conditioning.

ARTIST – ATHLETE

Bruce accentuated and considered himself first and foremost a martial artist and said that acting was his profession. As a martial artist he spent countless hours practicing and learning intensively with sheer dedication to elevate his skills to the highest level as possibly imaginable. Ted Wong one of Lees original personal students remembers Bruce telling him that he wanted to be the best martial artist in the world. Among the many top martial artists that worked out with Lee – Hayward Nishioka, the pan American gold medallist in judo, Gene Lebell, the greatest grappler of our time, top karate competitors Chuck Norris, Bob Wall, Mike Stone, Joe Lewis, and Jhon Rhee who's considered the father of USA Taekwondo – all agreed that Lee pound for pound may well have been the toughest 'dude' on the planet.

Bruce's research into the various forms of combat and training and conditioning methods lead him to cultivate an exceptionally effective art which he labelled 'Jeet Kune Do' – literally translated as 'The Way Of The Intercepting Fist'. Jeet Kune Do was a scientific Street-fighting method geared towards realistic Street-fighting.

Lee's keen analytical mind and mental acuity pushed him to delve into more deeper concepts and strategies in combat. A combination of rare mental and physical capability became the backbone of the exceptional skill in fighting he was able to acquire that has since been unequalled by his peers. Gene Lebell confirms "Bruce was very sharp, he was an innovator and the best at what he did".

Bruce had attained an imponderable level of proficiency that according to individuals who knew him it became near impossible to keep up with him, and almost frightening when training, so he spent a lot of time working out with Dummies where he could go all out full force without hurting anybody.

"I don't think anybody ever trained as hard as Bruce did, I don't think anyone in the world ever trained as the dedicated trainer as Bruce was" says Chuck Norris, who appeared with Bruce in the movie 'Way Of The Dragon'. Genetically endowed with extraordinary abilities Bruce was a physical specimen who proved what the human body was capable of achieving and enduring in terms of physical cultivation and perfection. He was absolutely insistent about physical fitness. Through his dedication to weight training and state of the art conditioning program Lee was able to cultivate an lethal physique that has since become his trade mark and mesmerised millions of people from martial artists, fans, Boxers, and the iron pumping fraternity. Only through dedication and hard work Lee was able to build himself into the superb physical specimen he was to become.

Truly Bruce Lee's physical attributes made him the extraordinary person he was, but there was more than just one facet to Bruce Lee which captured the more cognizant people's attention.

PHILOSOPHER – TEACHER

Its no secret, particularly in the martial arts circles, that Bruce Lee studied and had passion for Philosophy. As a matter of fact his art and philosophy were interrelated – his art of Jeet Kune Do was one of the vehicles he used to express his philosophy. Having influenced by great thinkers and philosophers – Krishnamurti, Allan Whatts and writers such as Norman Vincent Peale – Lee self educated himself and applied his philosophy to his art and life as a human being. The knowledge and deep understanding of human nature that he was able to acquire through researching, studying and reading largely contributed to his overall growth.

Above all, he was a thinker, this is what set him apart from others. Despite Lee's immense popularity around the world a large number of the public and fans are unaware of the fact that Lee was well versed in philosophy. One can more cogniscently see the mind set of Bruce Lee through his writings – apart from penning notes on fighting and training methods from the voluminous source material he had amassed during his short life period, he had penned philosophy essays and notes, notably from Krishnamurti, Zen and Allan Whatts works as well as psychology.

Bruce Lee expressed "a true martial artist should study philosophy and thereby come to understand himself and the ultimate meaning of combat". In short, what he really was trying to preach was by using a physical art (Jeet Kune Do) how a person can come to better understand himself and the world around him in addition to learning to fight.

Bruce was compelled to share his concepts and philosophy which he did via his teachings to his personal students, and later to a more wider audience via the medium of films. Bruce's teachings had an enormous effect on the many individuals who were fortunate to have studied with him. This was confirmed by Hollywood screenwriter and student of Lee's Stirling Silliphant – "He was not by trade a teacher of screenwriting or psychology, nor was he an ordained minister, and yet he was the greatest teacher I have ever known". Many of Lee's original students have gone on to say how Bruce's teachings changed their lives and had an impact on their lives – both as martial artists and as human beings.

Bruce Lee in his personal library

Quality not quantity was Lee's core teaching principle. His classes were kept very small and closed door. He believed that the Instructor or the JKD Coach should be like a Boxing coach in that he should pay very close attention to each individual student monitoring and developing the student in all facets of training. This is why he despised big classes and said Jeet Kune Do is not for every body because it requires one to be able to reach his genetic potential and independent thought and inquiry – a problem solving art – and many are not ready to delve deeper into the art, which is important in order to fully appreciate Jeet Kune Do.

Dan Inosanto remembers "I don't think anyone could teach as well as Bruce. He could get you emotionally involved. He didn't like to teach more than three students. In fact, in all his teachings, he never taught more than six students at one time."

Movie Icon

"He wanted to be a movie star" says James Coburn, "He wanted to make more money than Steve McQueen, per film, and did for one film anyway". One of Bruce's major goals in life was to give the gift of Kung Fu to the world. The only way he could reach the masses was via the medium of film. According to Linda Lee (Lee's widow) "Bruce never really conscientiously set out to achieve the world wide fame which, in fact, eventually came his way". That may partly be true, but Bruce was a very ambitious and motivated individual who lived for the martial arts. However, his main objective was to produce quality work, fame and fortune were by – products the results of hard work.

With his brilliant charm, enormous energy, and unmatchable talent he was able to express his character 'honestly expressing himself' which was so thrilling to the viewer. Millions of people all over the world put aside their troubles for a while to experience a truly unique experience as they lost themselves in the irresistible magic of his artistry – an experience they would never forget. The public were in awe of his skill, electrifying chemistry and magnetic screen presence that Lee was able to release and express on the screen.

Trough the medium of film Bruce Lee wanted to educate the public – he felt it imperative that he put his own unique stamp on each and every film. The early seventies was the era of inception of the Kung Fu boom and Lee was the single major influence behind the sudden growth of martial arts.

Enter The Dragon – Lee's last and only Hollywood movie – which made him an international star is regarded as the greatest martial arts movie of all time. The movie went on to gross over $200 million, when looking at the ratio of cost to [profit making, Enter The Dragon is perhaps the most successful movie ever. There has never been a single film with one star apart from Bruce Lee's Enter The Dragon which suddenly loomed like such a colossus over a genre. Bruce Lee's meteoric rise and untimely death marked the beginning as well as the end of a new genre world-wide. Bruce was literally on the edge of becoming the movie industry's hottest property, "There's no question that he would have been the biggest superstar if he had lived" says Fred Weintraub – the co-producer of Enter The Dragon.

Immediately after Lee's sudden death, there was much rage and grief across the world, crowds worldwide flocked to movie theatres to see his films in even greater numbers than before. Although he only completed four and a half films during his life time, these films continue to inspire and electrify millions and continue to be unsurpassable in terms of the unmatchable fight choreography, fighting action and magic that only Bruce Lee was capable of delivering. In 1992, finally it took Hollywood to realise that he really made a huge impact on a lot of people world-wide – that Lee was given a star on the Hollywood Walk Of Fame.

AN INSPIRATION

Above all, Bruce Lee strove to produce the best of quality work as possibly he could. His pursuit in life was towards improving the quality of his work –be it martial arts, training methods or film making- The dedication, determination, obsession and a goad of will power – ingredients firmly ingrained in him – drove him to reach goals beyond the reach of any one. "He was like the beacon, the source of energy that every body got something from" says James Coburn. Bruce set standards for all to follow. Apart from having an enormous impact on millions of ordinary people and fans, from all walks of life, Lee has had an incredible following and indelible impact on professional Boxers, the Bodybuilding fraternity – amateur and professionals – to athletes and of course martial artists all over the globe.

Many are intrigued by his artistry, fighting skills and incredible unmatchable physique, whilst others have been touched by his philosophy and teachings which they have absorbed to enhance their own lives as human beings.

Great legends and public figures have come and gone. Such unique human beings Marilyn Monroe, James Dean, Madonna, Muhammad Ali, Arnold Schwarzenegger, The Beatles, Elvis Presley who are all loved by the public are all recognised as the kings of their crafts and extremely gifted intriguing individuals. Of course, these legends have touched the lives of millions – then what is it that makes Bruce Lee shine out from the stars.

There's no incertitude to the fact that Bruce Lee's physical feats and qualities have been unsurpassable by his peers. Beyond the physical facet, Lee was able to integrate his philosophical concepts that allowed him to go beyond and cultivate himself on all levels as a human being. His ability to use his body in a most dynamic way – which was so intriguing – is clearly the most visible element that puts him apart. The intensity that was part of his dynamic personality fortifies the observer as it is released through the cinema screen.

His mind and innovations was the other factors that made him so unique and one of a kind. Lee's extraordinary and brilliant mind envisioned new and unique concepts that many use today but were unheard of back then. Bruce felt a strong sense of urgency subconsciously to achieve and reach goals in a short space of few years which takes thirty plus years.

Bruce Lee constantly strove to cultivate all facets with tremendous and painstaking care that were the sole of his personality and art which culminated his character. As the late Ed Parker put it "Bruce was one in a two billion." Since there always will be new and exciting personalities and idols cropping up – there will always be 'only one Bruce Lee'. Martial Artist, Streetfighter, Paragon of Health and Fitness, Philosopher, Teacher, and Movie Icon, the legacy of Bruce Lee continues to inspire people from all walks of life who seek the best within themselves.

JEET KUNE DO APPROACH

Jeet Kune Do has been labelled as 'The Pearl Jewel Of The Martial Arts'. Bruce Lee's passion for the martial arts lead him to formulate a lethal fighting method, which within it's confines comprised of various integral components that ultimately gives Jeet Kune Do 'life' and separates it from any other style system of fighting. These components of Jeet Kune Do form the Nucleus and roots which within their confines contain the imperative elements for success. Like the yin yang symbol, each component compliments each other and if the practitioner possesses the ability to examine, analyze and absorb theses essential facets, then he will be able to balance the total understanding of the most celebrated martial art developed.

Bruce described Jeet Kune Do as 'bare essential Street-fighting'. The ideology of realistic training approach introduced by Bruce Lee for martial arts has now in modern times been propagated all over by martial artists who now train with an edge of reality. The keen observer may see Jeet Kune Do as a composite of combat methods with an eclectic assortment of different techniques which can be found in various systems loosely strung together to form an effective fighting method. I must elucidate on the fact that Jeet Kune Do for Bruce was much more than just a form of fighting – rather Jeet Kune Do as a whole concept as Bruce would indicate to us(his personal students) is a composite of physical training methods, fighting concepts compromising of various core techniques,tactics, and combat strategies, backed up with scientific principles – and a philosophy which transcends the physical and technical elements.

BRUCE LEE'S TEACHING PRINCIPLES

Bruce was a perfectionist, his students were carefully chosen. The students that he did admit into his sheer, tight organisation, were on trial. Bruce preferred to have students with previous martial art training because it was easier for the student to appreciate more deeply what Bruce was trying to convey. He believed that the student should have the potential to be motivated to extend himself completely in hardcore strenuous activities to perform the techniques and exercises with internal intensity. According to Bruce, many students do not immolate or show their capability of truly and deeply understanding the hardcore approach to training – which is necessary in Jeet Kune Do – and physically dedicate themselves. There's no doubt he new that serious and sincere perspective students were difficult to come by, therefore unless the

LA Chinatown School located on 628 College Street. Larry Hartsell is on Bruce Lee's left side. Dan Inosanto is on Bruce Lee's right side

prospect proved his trust and worth, showed continued dedication along with reasonable improvement in the first six months would he accept him as a full member. As Dan Lee – one of Bruce Lee's top students and the first to be admitted into the L. A Chinatown school – recalls: "I think Bruce considered a persons sincerity in learning and willingness to train hard the two most important prerequisites…not until you had proven your sincerity and showed marked improvement from your persistent training did he admit you as a full member of his Los Angeles school".

Shortly after moving to Los Angeles area, Bruce decided to open up the now legendary Gym 'Jun Fan Gung Fu Institute' located on 628 college street in the Chinatown district. This secluded, anonymous looking place had no signs outside to identify it and strictly no visitors were allowed. Bruce decided to paint the windows red. The school was far from a commercial martial art school, it was a private place which one had to be invited and could not just walk in. These exclusive JKD closed door sessions were one of a kind which would be much talked about after Bruce's untimely death. Bruce said "I don't want too many in my organisation, the fewer students I have and the harder it is for anyone to join will give my club more prestige and importance. Like anything else, if it's too popular and too easy to join, people won't think too highly of it". Of course it takes a certain amount of discipline and dedication to push your body in order to reach your full potential, not many people are ready to put in the effort and input. This is why Bruce said Jeet Kune Do is not for everyone.

Initially he would test the students' persistence and dedication and he demanded total attention. Bruce's forte was one on one instruction. During the training sessions we would jump rope, perform supplementary exercises, develop our tools and practice certain new material or techniques that Bruce was teaching us. He was clear, precise and thorough. It wasn't unusual for the class to be supplemented by long lectures ranging from combat theories, training methods, and of course philosophy. It's intriguing how meticulous he was in his approach to teaching, he kept records on whom he was teaching and gave everybody a specifically prescribed supplementary training program tailored to each individuals needs.

As Bruce pointed out time after time "A teacher functions as a pointer to the truth, but not a giver of truth". The basic concept and principle behind his teaching was to help the students discover themselves physically, mentally spiritually, and to develop a 'discerning mind' not a dependant mind. This would be the phase where one begins to truly ascend to the higher aspects of the art. If the instructor lacks the ability to encourage exploration among his students, then the student becomes a clone of the master. Bruce insisted that an instructor is responsible for encouraging the students to explore both internally and externally finding out vulnerabilities and strengths, and the problem solving process which requires active participation by the students

Because teaching and coaching required a constant alert observation of the student, Bruce only taught a few people at any one time. The advantage of Bruce's teaching method was he was able to establish a direct relationship with the individual student, this way he could bring the best out of his students. Ian addition to training at the Chinatown school, a handful of us trained also at his house. Bruce seemed to enjoy these informal gatherings. During these private training sessions, Bruce would use us to experiment with new techniques and concepts, workout with shields, chi sau etc, and there was always good laughs to go with it. Here is an insight into Bruce's teachings from some of his personal students.

BRUCE LEE'S
TAO OF
CHINESE ɡunɡ Fu
USING NO WAY AS WAY ᵒ HAVING NO LIMITATION AS LIMITATION

Bruce Lee's original Board that hung at the LA School

"There is no one teacher that has made so great

impact on my training. Bruce liberated me from the classical training of blindly following fixed routines and believing that they represent the whole truth. He re-oriented my learning attitude and helped me understand that I should place my emphasis on the essence and spirit behind these movements, rather than vainly repeating form without any feeling. He left us suddenly, and yet his ideals, his philosophy, and his insights should remain fresh and alive in my mind forever". – Dan Lee

"When you think about it having the opportunity to study martial art from Bruce Lee, I've got to be one of the luckiest guys in the world, particularly since he taught me when I had no previous martial art experience. Bruce Lee usually only taught people that already had experience in martial arts. He took me in and made me not only his personal student, but also his friend". – Ted Wong

"Bruce knew that to be a good fighter you need to reach your maximum potential psychologically as well as physically. He said you need to "step through the door of insanity" and be able to come back. That's why moral character was so important to him. Without moral character you couldn't come back from that "insanity". Integrity was important to him because without it, the art degenerates into mere Street-fighting". – Jerry Poteet

"Instead of having you do 500 kicks, he would get you emotionally involved in ten kicks. He would always ask questions during training to get you to seek the truth about yourself…. he didn't believe in things like ippon kumite, one stage free sparring or three stage sparring, as they refer to it. He said "A drill has to be functional, it has to be close to reality". If it was not, he would throw it out. – Dan Inosanto

PRACTICE – LEARN – EXPERIENCE

Jeet Kune Do was never meant for mass distribution. After Bruce died there was no intention of having schools, teaching seminars and teaching openly. Unfortunately, the desire for JKD identification had resulted in the proliferation of unauthorised schools which forced Dan Inosanto to reach a wider scale by doing seminars to educate the public. Today there is a wider access to material available on Jeet Kune Do from books, video tapes and various authorised schools. So how does one experience Jeet Kune Do and most importantly how can the perspective serious student maximize his potential by enduring in the study and training methods of Jeet Kune Do.

Back in the mid-nineties the Jun Fan Jeet Kune Do Nucleus (which I was a founding member) with the sole intention of promoting, preserving and perpetuating the art and philosophy of Bruce Lee. The basic principle behind the formation of the Nuleus was to help the individuals who were interested in achieving excellence in Jeet Kune Do and educate the public. The Nucleus were responsible for compiling and bringing out a large chunk of Bruce Lee's original writings. Southern California is the birth place of Jeet Kune Do and the mecca of Jeet Kune Do activity – and as a matter of fact mecca of martial arts activity. I advise anyone who's seriously looking to travel the JKD path to find an instructor and research the art by finding as much material on it as possible and accumulate knowledge – which can then be absorbed and made to practical use. One must have three elements: the student should have skill in the performance, understanding and knowledge of the principles and should be able to trace his principal instructor directly to Bruce Lee.

Once the student has the fundamentals and structure firmly grasped, maximum training time should be devoted to honing the fighters physical qualities which is achieved through repetitively developing the tools and techniques until they become masterpieces. This is the very core of Jeet Kune Do training. At the same time the student must develop an understanding of the strengths and weaknesses of his fighting repertoire and be capable of formulating tactics and strategies that will work against any opponent is crucial. Learning, in Jeet Kune Do is a constant process of research and discovery, with no end, but more than merely a way of accumulating knowledge or techniques.

Ultimately the Jeet Kune Do student strives for constant experimentation to discover his own potential and tendencies, to find what best fits his stature and individual tendencies. This phase then becomes an extension path from the core structured base, a path we all must be proficiently knowledgeable about. Self examination, assessment and sheer dedication are prerequisites that will aid the student in his quest for elevating his potential. Although mastering techniques is an essential core of the Jeet Kune Do training, the exponent should be able to employ the intuitive and instinctive elements of his mind and body in combative training situations.

THE PATH FORWARD

The purpose of this book is a very direct and simple one. I present here a practical manual and guide which I surely believe can help any martial artist to accelerate his performance, skill, and understanding of Jeet Kune Do. I share with you many intermediate and advanced curriculum as developed, practiced and taught by my instructor Bruce Lee, in addition to the original material, I have shed light on modern concepts that I have included into my repertoire that have proven to be effective. I wish you all the best on your endeavour to experiencing the 'pearl jewel of the martial arts – Jeet Kune Do'.

1 — BRUCE LEE'S ENERGY DRILLS

Bruce Lee began teaching a modified form of Wing Chun shortly after he arrived in the United States. At times, he had to defend himself and his art both figuratively and literally against other Chinese martial artists. At that time, teaching kung-fu was very much a closed-door enterprise. Only ethnic Chinese were accepted as students. Bruce broke this taboo and would teach anyone who was sincerely interested in learning regardless if they were Chinese or not. This outraged many traditional kung-fu sifus. Some of them confronted him verbally. Others of them, however, confronted him physically.

Although he defeated his opponents in these confrontations, Bruce came away from these encounters with a growing awareness of the limitations of traditional Wing Chun. As he stayed longer in America, he became exposed to different martial arts systems and techniques. He began researching and analysing these methods, selecting and refining those which enhanced his combat effectiveness.

The path of self-discovery eventually led Bruce to establish his personal art of Jeet Kune Do. While the techniques of JKD went far beyond those found in Wing Chun, the key concepts and ideas of Wing Chun, along with some of its unique training methods, remain central to JKD. Some people have misunderstood Bruce's statements about personal freedom and self-expression in martial arts. They think that any technique they can make work for themselves is JKD. This is not true. JKD is a systematic method of approaching martial arts. The Wing Chun concepts which Bruce had learned became an important foundation for JKD. JKD is not just a grab bag of miscellaneous techniques.

Most traditional Chinese martial arts are known for their flowery, extended, circular techniques. Most systems have numerous forms. In this regard, Wing Chun is dramatically different. There are only three forms in WIng Chun. Wing Chun teaches the importance of maintaining the centerline, economy of motion, simultaneous blocking and striking, and practical application of techniques over formal execution. It is fast, direct and efficient. Wing Chun is especially known for its emphasis on 'energy' drills. These drills teach the student how to interpret an opponent's moves and then to use this information to defeat him.

Many of the people who sparred with Bruce thought he was psychic. He seemed to know what an opponent was intending to do and was already executing a countering technique before the opponent had even begun to move. Of course, Bruce wasn't really psychic. He did have supernatural speed and reflexes. But even more importantly, he was able to 'read' his opponent and anticipate his move. This ability was honed by Wing Chun sensitivity drills and training methods. He passed his methods on to his JKD students.

Once you have a technical 'know how' and begin to form a natural rhythm flow with your partner you can change and increase the tempo and speed of the drills to enhance the sensitivity within the drill. Constant drilling, mechanical precision and diligence are necessary prerequisites to achieving and developing a high level of skill and sensitivity which should be your primary goal. There are three stages you must go through in order to develop and make any technique work effectively. You must learn the technique; this should be done in a slow motion manner with a partner going through the movement slowly until you fully understand the technique and the mechanics behind it. The next stage is to train the technique on a partner with added elements of dynamic motion and resistance repetitively until it becomes a part of you.

In the final stage you must be able to apply the technique in a more combative mode and manner, ie in all-out sparring sessions. It may be easier to perform a technique against a totally cooperative partner, but trying to apply the same technique on somebody who is fighting you all-out and resisting you can be a whole new game. The stress level and reality increases, therefore it becomes necessary to progress our training to reality based scenarios to confide in our technical capabilities. Energy drills are a means to an end, not an end in itself, rather technical training methods used to develop certain attributes and skills that are vital in street fighting.

The most advanced method of sensitivity training in Wing Chun and JKD is known as Chi sau (sticking hands). Chi sau is a training process, it is not a set of movements. It uses all the techniques learned in forms and other exercises. It serves as a transition from formal training exercises to free fighting. The student learns to recognise opportunities and to strike effectively. Chi sau training begins with what is called dan chi sau (single sticking hand). Dan chi sau teaches how to make defense strong, it develops proper positioning and timing, and stance and structure.

What is important to keep in mind here is that these drills are to develop sensitivity to your opponent's energy. Don't use force or strength to overpower him. Feel his energy and respond to it using the minimal amount of your own energy to counter him.

Once the student has mastered dan chi sau he can progress to the full two-handed version. In dan chi sau the sequence of movements is limited and prearranged. This is not so in chi sau. Although it begins in a prearranged pattern it quickly becomes very individual and different. Each participant spontaneously responds to the energy he feels from his opponent and responds accordingly. Chi sau cannot be taught in a book or even a video. To learn it properly, the student must seek out a qualified instructor. The instructor must 'feed' the energy to the student to that he can feel it. However, to give the reader an idea of what chi sau looks like, I will demonstrate a session with an assistant.

There are some in the martial arts community who claim that chi sau is not a practical fighting technique and is therefore useless. I think they miss the point. These same critics would not discount the importance of running or weight training in martial arts. A martial artist doesn't run or do other aerobic exercise because he intends to have a foot race with an opponent. He does it to develop cardiovascular endurance which will help him in the ring or on the street. He doesn't do resistance training so that he can beat his opponent in a bench press contest. He does it to become stronger and to be able to hit and kick harder. In other words, the conscientious martial artist uses these supplemental methods to develop attributes which will make them better fighters. This is the purpose of chi sau as well. It helps the martial artist develop the attribute of sensitivity to an opponent's energy and thereby be a better fighter. If you don't think this is important, talk to some of the people who are still around who sparred with Bruce!

Chi sau is sticky hands exercise is a core training exercise method in Bruce Lee's Jeet Kune Do. The major factors in chi sau training is to cultivate sensitivity, contact reflexes, close range sticking techniques and flowing energy which enables you to feel your partner's force and learn to redirect and dissolve it instead of fighting force on force. During the course of the exercise you can control the partner's balance, pushing or pulling redirecting his force or attacks, trapping up his arms, short range punching, which requires razorsharp reflexes and speed.

Practice by rolling your arms in a harmonious co-ordinated manner; in the beginning stages pay very close attention to proper form, only when you have mastered the proper technique and eliminating any bad postures and habits should you start to experiment with more intricate combinations. It is very easy for the student to fall into the trap of sacrificing form over force. The student begins to apply jerky movements losing the 'plot' by carelessly rolling the arms all over the place instead of concentrating his efforts on proper technique and form.

Learn to relax and feel the slightest movement by your partner sensing the energy force and the direction the force is being applied. Once you have acquired the concept of being able to sense his intention and energy your response to counter accordingly will become almost instinctive. After prolonged repetitions drilling your reflexes will become sharper and yield mechanical and technical precision. When doing chi sau you can implement some of the following: a) pushing – technique is an excellent balance destroying tactic which usually surprises the adversary for a split second. Bruce could push, pull, tie up the arms and hit at will, offsetting the opponent's balance whilst performing chi sau. He became so good at this exercise that eventually he was able to do it blindfolded. The result of this was countless hours of awareness and sensitivity training; b) striking the center line – or outside; c) pulling both arms towards you, could head butt or knee strike; d) Jut sau and hit; e) tie up both arms by crossing them; f) various single and double arm trap and hit (straight punch, finger jab, backfist, chop, slap); h) Reflex Training – tactile awareness drill – partner drops both hands, you must lightly slap or palm his chest.

Chi sau is not fighting and it cannot and does not replace all-out combat. Rather it is a unique training method used by Wing Chun and Jeet Kune Do practitioners to accelerate the sensitivity and reflexes which are crucial elements in combat.

1. Larry is in double tan sau, his partner is in double fook sau position

2. Partner jut sao's pulling down on Larry's left arm then…

5. Partner pulls down on Larry's right arm, then…

6. …throws a left vertical punch this time, Larry counters with bong sau

One handed Harmonious Spring Drill

3. ...shoots a straight vertical punch. Larry responds by lifting left arm into bong sau

4. Return to starting position by jut sau again

7. ...partner jut sau's back to start position.

8. ...and the drill cycle continues as partner once again jut sau Larry's left arm

1. Larry and partner start off same as the last drill

2. Partner simultaneously pulls down on both of Larry's forearms then...

3. ...throws double vertical punches to the head. Larry responds with double bong sau...

Two-handed Harmonious Spring Drill

4. ...partner jut sau's both arms simultaneously, returning to starting position

5. Cycle continues as the partner once again throws double vertical punches...

1. Begin in a high outside reference position

2. Larry's partner pak sau's Larry's wrist simultaneously punching towards his face which is parried by Larry

3. Larry's partner feels the energy and wedges left arm upward, then...

Sliding Leverage Drill

4. Throws left vertical fist toward Larry's head while simultaneously pak sauing his left arm

5. He then wedges his right hand

6....and cycle continues on opposite side

1. This drill is called the Ball and Socket Princple – both partners face off

2. Partner throws a right-handed vertical punch which Larry counters with inward block

Swinging Gate Drill 1
(Ball and Socket Principle)

3. His partner rolls right arm at elbow in response to Larry's inward energy, pak sau's simultaneously striking backfist

3. ...which is blocked by Larry's inside parry

5. His partner how quickly reaches up with his left hand and pulls Larry's left arm down to lop sau downwards and striking with lead fist

1. This Drill begins with both partners in a reference position...

2. ie Larry blocking inward against partner's hook punch

Swinging Gate Drill 2

3. Partner feels the energy towards his forearm/wrist and pak sau's Larry's arm rolling his right arm into right backfist

4. …which Larry blocks inward with left arm applying sideway energy against the punch

5. Larry's partner collapses right arm circling…into right backfist while simultaneously lop sauing Larry's let arm which is an obstruction

BRUCE LEE'S ENERGY DRILLS

1. Partner's face each other in unmatched leads

2. Larry's partner throws left punch which Larry blocks with a lead bong sau...

3. Then lop sau's his partner's left arm and backfists towards his head...

4. His partner grabs Larry's backfist while collapsing his left elbow into a backfist...

Lop Sau to Lop Sau Drill

5. ...towards Larry's head simultaneously completing lop sau against Larry's right arm

6. ...cycle continues, Larry pulling partner's backfist whilst hitting backfist...

7. ...partner in motion ready to hit backfist

8. ...and lop sauing Larry's lead arm. Continue cycle

1. Both partners face off in matched stances

2. Larry's partner pak sau's against Larry's right arm while simultaneously throwing right punch which Larry counters with left bong sau...

3. ...Larry rolls into lop sau, and...

Bong Sau to Lop Sau Drill

4. ...backfist...

5. ...which is intercepted by grabbing Larry's wrist...

6. ...and pulls down lop sauing and simultaneously backfisting Larry's face which is grabbed. Continue cycle

Single Hand Chi Sau

1. Larry is in fook sau position, his partner is in tan sau position. Both facing each other in ready position

2. Partner pushes toward Larry's centre line with palm strike, Larry fook sau's against palm strike as soon as he feels the energy

3. Partner tan sau's against Larry's fook sau back into starting position and repeats the drill. Drill both hands as in training

Double Hand Chi Sau

1. Larry has left fook sau whilst his partner has his right arm in tan sau. Larry's right arm is in tan sau, his partner's left arm is in fook sau

2. The partner bong sau's against Larry's left arm and fook sau's against Larry's right arm

3. Exercise continues with both partners rolling back and forth. In JKD Bruce, instead of facing his partner, would do the chi sau from the onguard position with his lead foot forward

1. This drill demonstrates breaking out of the pattern. Partners begin standard chi sau drill

2. ... Continue drill feeling each other's energy, looking for an opening

3. Larry feints right hand, drawing his partner's right arm up...

Chi Sau to Lop Sau

4. ...which he now lop sau's against his partner's right arm smultaneously hitting backfist

5. ...which his partner grabs with left hand whilst keeping his right arm in bong sau position

6. ...continues lop sau cycle

2 — JKD Advanced Trapping Skills

The Wing Chun system is well-known for its 'trapping hands'. Bruce Lee thought highly of these methods and incorporated them into JKD. In Cantonese, trapping is called 'fan sao'. Bruce referred to trapping as "hand immobilisation attack (HIA)",

Trapping is not unique to Wing Chun or to JKD. Many martial arts incorporate trapping methods. Any practitioner of Filipino kali, Indonesian pentjak silat, Okinawan kyusho-jutsu/tuite, to name a few, will be proficient in some version of trapping. However, few systems have developed trapping to such a level of sophistication or have placed these methods to close to the heart of the art as in Wing Chun (and by extension, JKD).

Some people in recent years have questioned the value of trapping. They claim that trapping will not work in the rapidly changing, free-wheeling environment of actual combat. These criticisms are especially directed at 'compound' trapping. 'Compound' trapping is moving from one trap to another i a series of two or more moves.

I don't agree with the idea that trapping doesn't work in real combat. I think that the critics don't have a proper understanding of what trapping is and what it isn't. Firstly, one shouldn't think of a trap as a lock. A lock is intended to control a person (or one of his natural weapons) over a period of time. A trap, on the other hand, is intended to immobilise or check an opponent's movement for a brief moment. It's there for a beat of time and is gone. In that moment you can disrupt your opponent's momentum and rhythm. That makes it possible for you to take the initiative and press your own attack.

Secondly, although it may not be realistic to expect you can successfully execute compound traps, the training drills help you develop attributes which will make you a better. It improves your abilities to 'read' your opponent and feel the flow of his energy. As your perception improves, your reflexes will also improve. You will be able to react to your opponent faster and exploit his vulnerabilities.

Thirdly, as with many other techniques, in a real fight a trap will not look as crisp and pristine as it does in the gym. Regardless of what it looks like, it's still a trap if you have momentarily immobilised your opponent. I have found that trapping works well in the close range, especially from the tie-up position. It can be used both offensively and defensively.

In this chapter I want to focus on more advanced trapping drills. For this purpose I am assuming that the reader is familiar with basic trapping. Developing trapping skills in a continuum. It starts at a very basic level where the training partners practice single traps on each other. As the practitioner becomes more skillful, the drills become more complex.

As I have stated, I am not going to describe the single traps. There are many books and videos on the market which do this. I do want to briefly discuss the six 'reference points' used in describing trapping techniques. A reference point is nothing more than the relative position of the opponent's arms. In JKD, for the sake of convenience, we use six of these points.

In basic trapping, the practitioners begin with their arms already in contact in one of the reference points. In more advanced drills, the training partners begin in a fighting stance. They then use punches, kicks, or other methods to close the distance until they make contact. These drills are very free form. Each person is reacting to what his partner is doing. It therefore becomes impossible to prescribe what these look like in advance as each encounter is individual. Trapping should be part of every training session. Trapping is a fine motor skill which request constant attention and effort. No matter how sharp your skills are, they can always improve even more over time.

Bruce Lee knew that trapping becomes necessary when there is an obstruction between your attack and the target you are attacking, ie your backfist is blocked by the opponent. You can remove the obstruction by grabbing and pulling the opponent's arm simultaneously continuing your attack (backfist to the face) and scoring on the opponent in a split second. If applied correctly, trapping can be an essential took for the Jeet Kune Do fighter in a real fight.

Once the Jeet Kune Do student has a basic level of understanding and application of trapping hands he should immediately move onto compound trapping drills to cultivate finesse, speed, contact reflex skills and elevate his trapping skills to the highest level possible. At reaching this advanced level in your training you'll find the attributes developed through trapping will aid you in other areas of your fighting, make you extremely sharper and faster than you imagined was possible.

Bruce Lee taught trapping as part of his core program to his students. Trapping in Jeet Kune Do is no less or no more important element of training in Jeet Kune Do. It should be explored and emphasised to all who truly seek the best within themselves and become much more rounded martial artists and fighters.

Position One: High outside

Position Two: Low outside

Position Three: High inside

Position Four: Low inside

Position Five: High one side/one outside

Position Six: High inside/low inside

1. Both partners face off in onguard

2. Larry's partner throws lead punch to face which is intercepted by Larry's bil jee

5. Backfist counter which the partner blocks using outside wrist

6. Larry traps both arms pulling down

Compound Trapping 1

3. Larry pack sau's partners lead arm and throws lead straight punch which partner inside parries

4. Larry disengages and grabs left hand, lop sau's whilst rolling right arm into...

7. ...quickly using left arm to trap both of partner's arms and throws right punch face

8. ...and finishes with elbow strike to face

1. Both partners face° off in right onguard stance

2. This time Larry initiates by pak sau'ing partner's lead arm simultaneously hitting vertical punch to face. Partner inside parries

3. ...Larry wedges (in combat hit finger jab to eyes) which partner obstructs with outside of wrist

Compound Trapping 2

4. ...so Larry pak sau's the obstruction with right hand simultaneously throws left vertical punch...

5. ...and right vertical punch as Larry pulls the partner off balance into a punch

ADVANCED TRAPPING SKILLS

1. Both partners square off in right onguard stances

2. Larry's partner jabs low to Larry's stomach. Larry pak sau's and right punch face – partner inside parries

3. Larry wedges outside partner's left parry and rolls into right backfist…

4, …but changes into right pak sau and left punch to face

Compound Trapping 3

5. ...which is inside parried by partner with right hand

6. Larry wedges partner's parry for sneaking in a finger jab to eyes, which is obstructed

7. Larry pak sau's partner's right hand downward and punches with right vertical fist...

8....then inside pak's with left hand simultaneously strikes vertical punch to chest

ADVANCED TRAPPING SKILLS

1. Start p osition, both partners in ready right onguard positions

2. Partner throws low lead jab which Larry counters with ha pak...

3. ...then quickly executes low pak sau with left hand and simultaneously throws right backfist which is inside blocks

Compound Trapping 4

4. Larry pak sau's partner's left arm at the same time hits right vertical fist into partner's chest

5. Then uses right gum sau (pinning hands) to trap both arms as he strikes with left punch to face

6. ...quickly checks the partner's right arm as he strikes a right horizontal elbow side of the face

ADVANCED TRAPPING SKILLS

1. Starting position – right onguard stance

2. Larry counters partner's low jab with low ha pak as he punches with high right vertical punch...

3. ...then shoots a left high punch to face sliding across the top of partner's left arm

Compound Trapping 5
(Straight blast)

4. ...then follows up with a straight right vertical fist punch to chest...

5. ...left vertical fist punch to chest...

6. ...and finishes the opponent off with a right vertical fist to chest. You may apply all punches to the face alternatively

ADVANCED TRAPPING SKILLS

1. Both partners face off right onguard stance

2. Larry engages with a low jab which is outside low parried by partner

3. ...Larry pak sau's with left hand simultaneously firing a lead punch to the face, partner inside parries

4. ...Larry cuts on the outside line

Compound Trapping 6

5. ...to lop sau and fire right punch which is again inside parried by partner

6. ...Larry pak sau's partner's parrying arm and attacks with right backfist, again partner parries

7. ...finally lap sau's partner's left arm

8. ...and hits right backfist to the face

2. Larry steps in throwing a low jab to connect to low reference point to draw a reaction

3. ...now he pak sau's partner's lead arm to throw a backfist

1. Both partners square off in right unguard stances

Compound Trapping 7

4. ...but the partner is quick and raises his lead arm to stop him; now they are in high outside reference point

5. ...Larry quickly counters again by a lead pak sau and lead punch, partner inside parries

6a. Larry traps partner's both arms pinning them with his left and hits right punch face

6b. Alternatively he can trap both arms by circling right elbow and gum sau and punch with left

ADVANCED TRAPPING SKILLS

Compound Trapping 8   NPM Principle

1. Partners square off

4. Larry goes to the outside line with a left punch to face

2. Larry attacks with a lead straight punch, partner inside parries with lead hand

5. ...and traps with his left hand partner's left hand

3. ...Larry pak sau's and hits straight lead punch which partner meets with inside left parry

6. ...to complete a second hit, lop sau and right backfist to the face

Compound Trapping 9

1. Both partners square off

2. Larry attcks with left finger jab, opponent outside parries

3. Larry completely changes the line of the attack by throwing right finger jab which opponent blocks

4. ...Larry pak sau's and hits right punch which the opponent tan sau blocks

5. ...Larry sees an opening and fires in a left punch to the body

ADVANCED TRAPPING SKILLS

1. Opponent faces Larry in the kicking range

2. Larry's opponent throws a rear round kick. Larry counters by sidestepping and riding the kick to asorb its energy

3. Larry fakes a finger jab to the eyes to distract opponent

6. Larry lop sau's opponent's parrying arm

7. ...and throws a right backfist or hammerfist

Compound Trapping 10

4. ...and slides in with a low shin kick to bridge the gap

5. Opponent throws lead punch to body which Larry pak sau's and hits lead to face

8. ...and a left finger jab to the throat whilst maintaining a double arm check...

9. ...and finishes him off with a right horizontal elbow whilst trapping with left arm

ADVANCED TRAPPING SKILLS

Once you reach a standard level in trapping skills, you can free flow 'spar' with your partner to take your skills to an even higher level. You and your partner will learn to react instantly and improve your reflexes and speed of reaction. In this sequence Larry and Sifu Dan demonstrate an advance free flowing trapping. Trapping in the hands of a skilled opponent can be dangerous and effective in controlling and neutralising the opponent.

1. Larry inside parries Dan's

2. ...punch

3. Dan throws left punch which Larry parries

6. ...Larry pak sau's and hits right punch which Dan parries

4. ...Larry pak sau's Dan's left arm

7. ...Larry wedges

5. ...and throws left finger jab which Dan inside parries

8. ...lop sau's

One and Three Inch Punch

One of the most dramatic techniques which Bruce used in public demonstrations and social gatherings was the one- (and three-) inch punch.

As impressive as these were for onlookers, it had even more impact (pun intended) on those of us who had the experience of being on the receiving end of Bruce's punch. Bruce, being a relatively small and wiry person, loved to demonstrate on larger people. Because I was one of his physically larger students, I found myself 'volunteering' to assist him in these demonstrations on more than one occasion. If observers were impressed at the sight of a large person being propelled several yards backward by a barely imperceptible punch which only travelled one inch before striking its target, let me assure you that it was even more impressive to be on the receiving end and experience the tremendous amount of power generated.

The key to successfully learning this technique is to begin from a proper position and to shift the weight through the hips focusing all of your power with the punch. You need to be relaxed to be able to explode through the point of contact.

The one and three inch punch can be very useful in close range and grappling range – ie after trapping up the opponent's arms you may end up too close to punch. This allows you an opportunity to strike the opponent from very close range using the one or three inch punch exploding through his chest and still knocking him back. I have personally seen Bruce knock a heavyweight back feet away using this basic but intriguing close range punch which didn't take much time for the guy to realise that he shouldn't mess with Bruce. This happened back when I took Bruce to a clothes shop in Beverly Hills and this big coloured guy heavyweight was winding Bruce up. He obviously did not know what tremendous power Bruce was capable of generating – even though he only weighed 135 pounds and being of a very small stature. Anyway, to cut a long story short, the guy became a believer.

Various training methods and exercises can be implemented and utilized into your training routine such as the use of the grip exerciser and wrist curls with dumbells which can increase your punching prowess and explosiveness. In developing the one and three inch punch it is important to utilize and make use of your hips and waist. Learn to put the whole of your body behind the blow, do not shove or push but explode punching 'through' the opponent's chest or the partner's target area. Have a partner hold a Yellow Pages book in front of his chest or a focus glove and practice from the onguard position. A guiding principle behind this punch is that the energy starts from the feet and trunk which is the root to power and flows right through with the final point being the fist. This can be compared to the concept of water or electricity flowing through the channel from the feet exploding through the target.

There is nothing magical about this technique. The secret to its mastering is constant practice. You must develop through countless repetitions, explosiveness and shifting of your body into the punch. The essence of the punch is speed of initiation, power, snap and body position.

1. Starting position, application of three inch punch

2. Larry pak sau's and straight vertical punch

3. Larry pak sau's inside with left hand…

4. …and is too close to withdraw to puch so uses close range three inch punch which propels his opponent feet away

ADVANCED TRAPPING SKILLS

1. Have a partner hold a Yellow Pages book in front of his chest

2. Your open fingers should be touching the book with rear heel raised

3. Note how Larry's body shifts to transfer all his weight into the punch

4. ...which knocks the partner back feet away

1   2   3

This simple exercise requires the partner to hold a sheet of paper. Note the relaxed position of Larry's wrist in photo 1. He then snaps into the target then retracts to starting position.

1   2   3

Practice the three inch punch on a focus glove. These phtographs show close up how you snap into position using the last three knuckles

3 — WOODEN DUMMY TRAINING

Aunique piece of training equipment used by Wing Chun and JKD practitioners is called the 'mook yan jong' in Cantonese. In English this translates to 'wooden man'. Although wooden training dummies are used in other systems of Chinese martial arts (Choy Lay Fut is a notable example), it is students of Wing Chun who have used it most extensively and developed its practice to the most sophisticated level. It was one of the most essential pieces of which Bruce Lee used in his quest for technical perfection.

The wooden dummy has a wooden trunk approximately six feet tall and approximately 12 inches in diameter. Two arms project from the trunk just below neck level. A third arm projects from the trunk at waist level. A leg extends forward from the lower portion of the trunk. Bruce made several modifications to the traditional dummy to make it more realistic. One of these was to have a channel beneath the head to simulate a neck. He also experimented with spring-loaded arms and legs in various configurations.

Although the dummy does not replace a live sparring partner, it serves as a valuable substitute when a partner is not available. In addition, you can apply full force techniques against the dummy without damaging it. The same techniques against a live opponent would result in serious injury. Bruce felt that the mook jong was one of the best pieces of apparatus to aid in cultivating blocks, simultaneous parrying and hitting, pulling techniques, trapping and striking. He believed that training on the dummy honed his skills, elevating them to a razor-sharp level, improving his speed and explosiveness to an even higher level.

One of the key elements to using the dummy to its maximum effect is to focus on the angle of entry and the angle at which techniques are executed. As you study the photographs on the following pages, pay particular attention to the angle of the demonstrator's body relative to the mook jong and to shifts in body position during the transition from one technique to another.

Traditionally, the mook yan jong set was considered to have 108 techniques, although the exact number could vary among practitioners. This complete set was broken down into several series of movements. The student would advance to the next series only after having mastered the previous series.

Training on the mook jong is such a complicated and intricate subject that a whole book could be devoted to it alone. In fact, there have been books written (and videos made) on this topic alone. I am not therefore going to try to cover the entire set. Instead, I am going to present the first 50 moves. In Hong Kong during the days Bruce was training with Yip Man, the first 50 movements contained the most basic and essential movements. As the student progressed to the more advanced movements, he was allowed a degree of leeway for individual expression. However, the first 50 movements are performed virtually identically by all Wing Chun students.

Author standing next to Bruce Lee's original wooden dummy. Inherited by Dan Inosanto

When you are working the mook jong you should always imagine that you are executing the techniques against a live opponent. Your practice should always be alive and dynamic. You should never be stiff and mechanical. Bruce would free-lance on the dummy. He would intuitively mix techniques using his own creativity and imagination. You should do the same and make your own path. When Bruce worked on the dummy it sounded like someone was firing a machine gun; his speed, explosiveness and skill was just incredible. Although it is useful to master the set as presented, it is important not to be bound by it. Your imagination is the most important training tool you have at your disposal. Experimentation was the cornerstone to Bruce's approach to training. You should practice individual techniques on the dummy. You can punch, block, kick, trap and practice entry to throws. As your proficiency improves, you can begin to incorporate more combinations into your training. The JKD four-corner defense, simultaneous strike and defense, shin kick entry, low oblique kick etc, should all be part of your training regimen.

It's impossible to prescribe a 'one size fits all' approach to mook jong training. How much any given person should train depends on what skills that person already has and what his or her strengths and weaknesses are. If you have never trained on the dummy before I recommend that you train on it for at least 20 minutes per session, and at least three days per week. Once you have become familiar with the mook jong you can adjust your training appropriately. Today many Jeet Kune Do exponents tend to neglect or spend too little time on the wooden dummy. You will discover and fulfil your

potential as a martial artist as your skill and repertoire is raised by implementing regular wooden
dummy training into your program.

The following original JKD set (for the first time ever
in a book) is as Bruce taught to us and which has
never before been presented before. I have added an
entry to bridge the gap before beginning the first
series.

First Series

2. ...fake bil jee

1. Ready stance onguard

3. ...enter with low side kick

2. Left lop sau with right palm strike

3. Right hand jut sau neck

1. Double inide sliding wedge with right hand slightly ahead

4. Right bong sau between arms as hips twist to right

5. Right tan sau with left horizontal palm strike to middle...

6. Double gong sau to right

8. Left tan sau with right horizontal palm hit to mid level

9. Double gong sau to left...

7. Qun sao to right, low bang sao with high tan sau simultaneously

10. Left tan sau, right hun sao

11. Right vertical palm smash to face, left jut sao

12. Right hand circles down between arms counter clockwise

14. Double bil jee

15. Double jut sau...

13. Double jut sao...

16. Tak sao...

Second Series

17. Starting position is with both hands inside, left leading...

18. Double inside sliding wedge with left hand forward...

19. Right lap sao with left neck jut (pull)...

20. Left bong sao between arms...°

22. Double goang sao (outside-inside hit) on right...

23. Kun sao to left with low bong and high left tan sao simultaneously...

21. Left tan sao with right horizontal palm strike to mid level...

24. Right outside tan sao with left low horizontal palm strike...

25. Low right goang sao with high outside left tan sao

26. Left hung sao (circling hand) with right tan sao...

28. Double jut sao...

29. Double tak sao upward

27. Right hung sao and jut with right hand, then left horizontal palm strike

30. Return to double jut sao...

31. Double tak sao (upward palm strike)

WOODEN DUMMY TRAINING

Third Series

32. Inward palm parry...

33. Inward palm parry with left...

36. and back...

37. Into horizontal reverse chop...

34. Inward palm parry with right

35. Left hand slides forward...

38. Left jut sao (grab) as right hand punches...

39. Left pak sao...

41. Slide forward with diagonal chop

42. Right jut sao (grab) with left punch to midline...

40. Right hand circles across top of arm...

43. moving into...

44. Double palm jut sao...

45. Double tak sao

Fourth Series

45. Starting position...

46. Right bong sao to lower arm...

47. Left pak sao...

48. Right sut sao (vertical chop) underarm

49. Right jut tek (kick) holding right bong sao position

50. Double gong sao to left

51. Right pak sao...

52. Left horizontal chop under arms...

55. Move inward

56. Between arms...

53. Left jut tek

54. Double goang sao to right...

57. Into double horizontal palm strike to ribs...

58. Raise hands between arms...

60. Double jut sao…

61. Double tak sao

59. Into double palm strike to face…

Fifth Series

62. Start from goang sao...

63. Circle hung sao to right...

64. Circle hung sao to left...

66. Right bong sao high and between arms...

67. Right jik tek with right tan sao and left horizontal palm strike...

65. Circle hung sao back to left...

68. Scrape down and stamp opponent's foot

69. Double goang sao on left

70. Circle hung sao to right…

72. Circle hung sao to right...

73. Left bong sao between arms...

71. Circle hung sao to left...

74. Left jik tek with left tan sao and right palm strike

75. Double goang sao to left...

76. Double goang sao on the right...

77. Circle hung sao to left...

78. Double jut sao and strike to face with right...

79. Circle right down between arms…

80. Double jut sao and right horizontal palm strike to face

81. Double tak sao to finish

4   JKD SPARRING TACTICS

Although Bruce was always experimenting with new and innovative training methods he always emphasised the importance of sparring to his students. He often compared martial artists who didn't spar to swimmers who never went into the water. Bruce believed that students had to test their skills by sparring. In the last decade the phenomenon of No Holds Barred (NHB) competition has demonstrated and propagated the need for more realistic training.

Jeet Kune Do students need to evaluate their training and the foremost key being the need for a balance of all the elements whilst putting extra emphasis on sparring or full contact fighting. Much of the techniques that are taught in martial arts are just a hypothesis, only until we test them in a realistic form of sparring or situation can we clearly see the validity and effectiveness of these techniques. As much as we may find certain techniques and methods that 'look good' we must strip down to the essential with the intention of finding the most practical way of applying them in a full contact manner, otherwise we can easily fall into the trap of ingraining a false sense of confidence.

Sparring, then, can be a laboratory for the martial artist to experiment with which techniques work and which don't. Many students are indoctrinated in certain schools of thought, schools that have their students practice forms and unrealistic techniques which have no real bearing on combat. Sparring realistically whilst retaining a margin of safety – to avoid serious injury – against an uncooperative, aggressive partner is crucial in testing your repertoire and skill. It gives the student a more realistic tool with which to evaluate his own skills.

A particular student may become very proficient at drills which control the variables, but is unable to spar effectively against a live opponent. Sparring makes unique demands on a fighter. Once he is confronted by an opponent who hits back, the fighter finds himself exerting himself physically more. Remember the saying 'No pain, no gain'. One must put himself in high-pressured, uncomfortable training situations in order to appreciate the prodigious benefits that all-out sparring can bring. Hardcore sparring rounds which demand a high level of fitness and mental toughness will leave you physically and mentally drenched.

It is important and imperative that the students are able to test their skills in a safe, controlled environment of a school under the supervision of a qualified instructor. Many beginners tend to shy away from sparring for the fear of getting hit, or lack confidence in their ability to find out what works or doesn't work for themselves. Fear is a normal part of the human psyche. Fear helped our ancestors to survive by warning them they were in danger. While it is an essential part of human nature, the student must learn to control and channel his fear productively. We all have what are known as 'comfort zones'. but to improve in any walk of life, to find and conquer our fears we must get up and push ourselves to the limits and not be scared of trying new and effective methods and approaches. Methods that will make us better than what we are today. Sparring is a vehicle ideally suited to this task.

In the old days (LA Chinatown School), Bruce had us geared up with boxing gloves or open hand gloves (that Bruce adapted from Japanese kempo/kendo and which he made famous in 'Enter the Dragon') body armour, baseball shinguards, Navy headguards and groin cups and mouthpieces. He wanted his students to experience real total combat so that when a real situation arises, they would not 'freeze' when high pressure was placed on them. The Jeet Kune Do student should be mentally conditioned along with his tenacity and confidence cultivated to prepare him for hardcore sparring. Once you enter the realm of sparring you'll encounter many new 'truths' in combat.

At the Chinatown School we were taught many sparring drills designed to develop a sense of distance, evasiveness, timing, counter-attack and interception skills. Both training partners would face off in the unguard position with 16oz boxing gloves practicing 'catch/evade and return drills', fake and feinting drills to advance tactics of drawing an attack. These specialized drills pave the way for more hardcore sparring with the principal aim of going all-out. This phase is when you develop your conditioning, attack and defense strategy and tactics, footwork and timing, and what Bruce believed to be an essential element/ingredient 'killer instinct'. This killer instinct puts the fighter in possession of a tool of considerable value. There are a number of approaches to sparring. Any beginner of course, should begin with more controlled drills. They should begin with basic hit-and-response drills. As their ability improves, more combinations of attack and response are introduced and practiced. This leads to all-out freestyle full contact sparring. In the beginning you may feel clumsy and find it awkward with weighty, bulky gloves on. Some first timers are overwhelmed by getting hit with a barrage of punches because they've never been hit before or experienced impact. But with each successive sparring session it will only be a matter of time before you begin to fit into the sparring environment.

Certain techniques and tactics such as the JKD straight blast can be tested and drilled in a sparring mode. According to Dan Inosanto, Bruce Lee always reverted to the straight blast whenever he was serious about a fight. This was one of his greatest assets – rapid assault tactics – which worked, much to his delight against even a bigger opponent. The concept behind the straight blast drill is to overwhelm your opponent with a flurry of lightning-fast punches, breaking his balance; simultaneously the guy should be peddling backwards or fall flat on the floor. This tactic should also be effectively employable in sparring rounds as a transition into close-range fighting.

Another excellent sparring method is the 'clinching and hitting'. This is when you and your partner are in close tie-up boxing position. This is the range when the boxer learns to take and give heavy punishment thus learning to eliminate the fear of getting stung and absorb heavy punishment. It is essential you and your partner wear a mouthpiece and headguard along with boxing gloves. During drilling or rounds you can grab neck shoulder push/stop, block, push etc to make it more productive.

Protective gear for full contact JKD sparring. Headguard, hand wraps, mouthpiece, shin guards, boxing gloves. Not shown is a groin protector inasmuch as Sifu Hartsell's personal cup was too large to fit into this frame.

Intercepting is a core principle of Jeet Kune Do. Full contact stop-hit drills against a partner (who is geared up with gloves, shinguards, body armour etc.) will help you develop fine sense of distance and improve your timing. In the beginning drill on various stop hits, working your way up to the level where your partner attacks in combination unlike the pre-set drills.

In sparring you must be in total control of your emotions. Concentrating on the job at hand. Completely obscuring and obliterating all past negative emotions that may impede your total control over yourself. While the fighter punches himself to his limits physically, he is also pushing himself emotionally. He is learning to control his anger. An angry fighter is a person not in control of himself. When he makes a mistake, instead of getting upset or angry he should ask himself what errors lead him to make the wrong move and how can the problem be solved. Learning is two-fold – you learn from your mistakes as well.

1. Begin with looped end

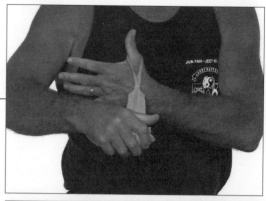

2. Insert thumb and wrap oer back of hand...

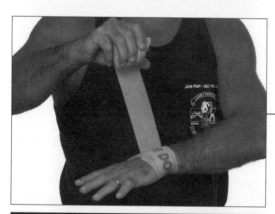

3. ...then twice around wrist

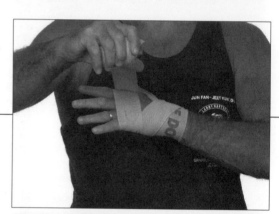

4. Bring it across back of hand and knuckles...

7. ...finally looping over...

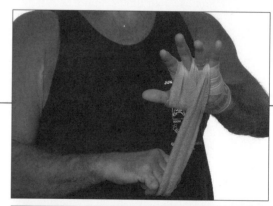

8. ...and down between little finger...

5. ...and then loop over and down between index and middle fingers...

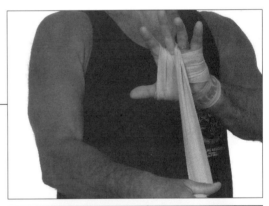

6. ...and then continue looping between middle fingers

9. Then wrap across palm...

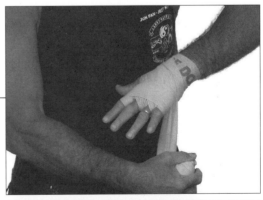

10. ...and across knuckles and...

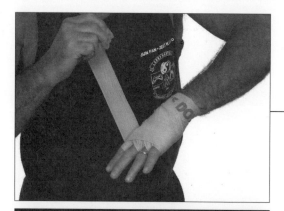

11. ...wrist

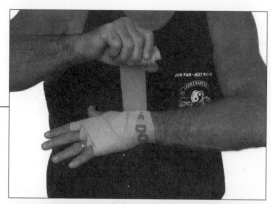

12. ...

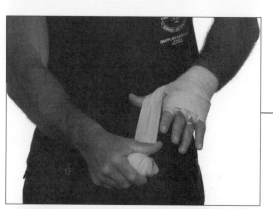

13. Bring wrap around thumb...

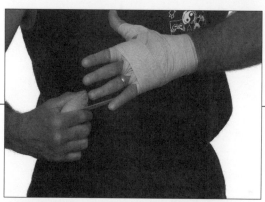

14. ...and wrap remaining length around...

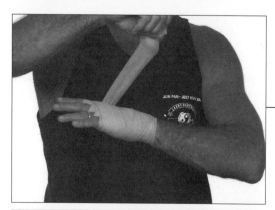

17. ...wrist...

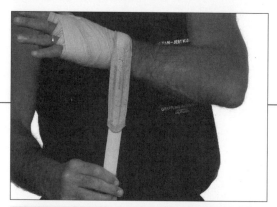

18. ...over the wrist...

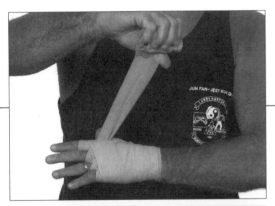

15. ...bringing it inside the thumb...

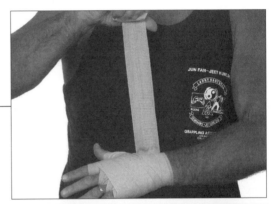

16....knuckles and outside...

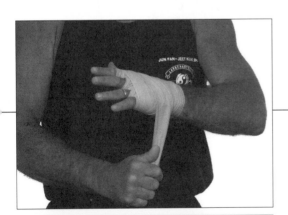

19. ...and finish by sticking the velcro together

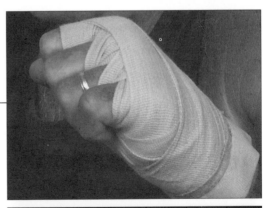

20. Close up of wrapped hand.

1. Both partners in original stances

2. Figher A (on right) slips jab thrown by fighter B (on left)

3. Then slips outside as B throws a cross

The primary purpose of this Drill is to develop evasive skills in movement. In the beginning the partner attacks in a rhythmic, mechanical way, later to progress further and develop speed, reflex and timing the attacker/coach should break the rhythm in between the punches. This will also force the defensive fighter to be on alert at all times.

Evasive Drill/Tactics

4. B throws a left hook to which A bobs and…

5. …weaves to the outside

6. B responds with a right hook which A bobs and…

7. …weaves to the outside

JKD Sparring Tactics

1. Both partners face off in onguard stance

2. Fighter A slips outside of fighter B's jab

3. Then A counters with a rear cross which B catches and shoulder rolls

Learning to counter attack just as your partner is recovering from his own attack should be a necessary part of your tactical training. Your attacking motions should bring you back to a good position, from where you can easily be defensive if the opposition lands a counter-attack suddenly. In sparring learn to keep yourself covered when attacking because it is not uncommon for the opposition to counter your attack with his own flurry of punches. Evasive tactics should be combined with punishment in sparring to learn to be defensive and offensive at the same time.

Evade and Counter Drill/Tactics

4. B then counters by throwing a cross which slips to the left side this time

5.... and left hooks to head. (Note: B uses his boxing glove in the beginning stages. Later works way up to safe contact to head)

6. A then slips to the inside of B's hook punch

7. ...and low hook punches into B's ribs...

8. ...and quickly throws an overhead right to B's head

9. B counter attacks with right hook which A bobs and weaves to the outside...

10. ...and uppercuts to B's exposed stomach...

11. ...anbd finishes offwith a left hook

1. Partners square off

2. A uses low leg wing block against B's low hook kick simultaeously punching with straight right...

ATTACK STRATEGY

a) You can strike as your opponent is planning to initiate or preparing to attack or advance

b) You can strike when the opponent is in the midst of his attack

c) You can attack when you think the opponent loses his concentration for a while

d) You can quickly counter strike as soon as the opponent has landed his attack, ie kick which missed due to your footwork or blocked by you

Stop and Counter Drill/Tactic

3. A follows up with counter combination attack left hook…

4. …right cross…

5. …low hook kick to thigh whilst keeping his lead hand in front checking just in case the partner punches

1. Starting posotion for reaction drill with coach on outside. Coach taps one arm to indicate which punch to throw

2. Student throws left uppercut if coach touches left

3. If coach touches right, student throws right uppercut

Reaction Drill

4. ...or right cross...

5. ...or left hook. The purpose of this drill is to develop timing, speed and reaction time

1. Both partners square off

2. Fighter B uses leg wing to clock fighter A's right hook

3. A throws low inside round kick as B lands in fighting stance...

4. ...and blocks A's low hook kick...

Entering to Clinch Drill

5. A attcks with left knee which B stops with both cross hand block

6. ...then rapid knees right...

7. ...and left combination are thrown which B stops...

8. Both fighters end up in close range clinch position

Boxing from the Clinch Drill/tactics

1. Fighters begin in tie-up position

2. A pushes B off with forearm

3. ...then hooks to B's head which B covers...

6. right cross...

4. and counters with right cross...

7. left uppercut...

5. left hook...

8. and back in the tie-up position

1. From the tie-up position

2. Fighter A shifts to right pulling B off balance to set up right knee

3. B counters with inside pak sao and left vertical punch

Sparring and boxing from a clinch is an excellent method of training to build confidence in close range punching and taking punishment. You can push, shove, pull, grab and punch. Make the drilling more productive by moving around in a clinch and try to look for or create an opening. Remember to wear a headguard and mouthpiece as well as 16oz boxing gloves to prevent serious injury to yourself and your partner.

Boxing from the Clinch Drill/Tactics

4. right u ppercut...

5. left uppercut...

6. left hook...

7. right cross...

1. Both fighters face off in fighting positions

2. Fighter B feints right high cross

False attacks and feints are effective tactics to gain distance – close the gap – from where you can land a barrage of explosive attacks. One can effectively confuse the opponent and baffle him before launching your attack and score. False and feint attacks are workable tactics against an opponent who seems to have a strong defence. You can feint to draw a reaction from the opponent to see how he reacts – test him out before committing to any type of attack or tactic.

Feint Entry Attack Drill/Tactic

3. Drawing A to raise his guard high up

4. …then B kicks to inside thigh on the open line

5. Fighter B quickly gets out of range by shifting into a right lead stance

JKD Sparring Tactics

1. Larry and partner start off same as the last drill

1. Both fighters face off in onguard stances

2. Fighter B fakes a low punch or tckle to induce A to drop guard

4. ...withdraws to a guard position just out of reach...

Low Feint Entry Drill/Tactic

Distance plays an imperative role in feinting tactics. If you start throwing a fake too close the opponent may be able to counter attack fast. If you're too far you might not get a reaction at all or you may not be able to reach him with the actual real attack. Always 'feel' and regulate the gap between your partner and yourself.

5. ...and kicks to the thigh (to the groin in the street) – but for training purposes use the inner thigh

1. Partners face each other in fighting stances

2. Fighter B fakes a left front knee to induce A to drop his guard and...

3. ...then quickly changes line of attack...

OBJECTS OF THE FEINT

a) To force the adversary to open the line in which you intend to attack

b) To lengthen the adversary's reaction time whilst you close the gap/distance or attack

c) To invite a reaction block/parry to engage and trap arm and hit/lock

d) To confuse and intimidate the adversary, baffle him totally keeping him on the defensive

e) To increase the chances of 'scoring' on the adversary who is very defensive

Low Feint Entry Drill/Tactic

4. ...by throwing a low hook kick to thigh...

5. ...Now that the distance has been closed into punching range, B follows up with a left cross...

6. ...and right uppercut

1. Fighters face off

2. Fighter B fakes right kick causing fighter B to shift to his left...

3. Fighter B changes line of attack

DRILL/EXERCISE

Pair up with a partner moving around like you're sparring. Throw fakes with your hands just to get reactions. In this drill the partner does not counter attack rather reacts to your fakes – in between throw a real attack. The objective is to see how he reacts. Does he slip, parry, move, to your feints. Later you should be able to apply these tactics when sparring all-out. Sparring without the necessity to defend oneself can at best be classified as a one-sided drill. You must progress to attacking whilst the partner must try to counter attack.

Closing the Distance Drill/tactics

4. ...opening him up to a groin kick...

5. ...into boxing/punching range – overhand right...

6. ...left uppercut

1. Starting position, both fighters face off

2. Fighter B drops lead hand down to draw A to attack on the highline

3. Fighter A throws right cross which B counter attacks with right low cross to body...

Against someone who primarily bases his strategy on stop-hitting and counter attacking, then 'Drawing an Attack' tactic has an solution. Such as purposely opening up exposing an area inviting the adversary to take the lead and lure him into attacking you. The main objective is to bait him or lure him into a trap – where you can surprise him counter attacking in a single stroke or rapid combinations.

Invitation Drill/Tactic 1

4. ...and left shovel hook to ribs

JKD Sparring Tactics

1. Opponents face off

2. This time B drops his rear right hand

3. ...inducing A to throw left hook as he thinks fighter B has left himself open

DRILL EXERCISE

Square off with a partner – with the appropriate gear – boxing gloves, mouthpiece etc. Expose any one or two defensive corners as to tell the partner to take advantage and attack the vulnerable area. As soon as your partner attacks at the target area, parry and hit simultaneously or intercept him with a punch before his attack reaches you. Start moving around as if you're both sparring. Drill for a couple of minutes and change roles. This drill is excellent for your reflexes, timing, speed and alertness

4. ...B bobs and weaves to the outside as he sees the hook coming...

5. ...then counter attacks with low right hook on the open line which is left open by A

6. ...and high left hook punch to the face for a knockout

1. Starting position

2. Fighter B lifts guard on purpose to expose ribs...

3. Fighter A attacks with left round kick, which...

4. Fighter B counters with a right straight intercepting punch by stepping in to off balance him...

Invitation Drill/Tactic 3

5. ...and to get inside his opponent throws left uppercut or shovel hook...

6. ...and right overhead punch to face

JKD Sparring Tactics

1. Both opponents in onguard positions

2. Fighter B drops his left guard down

3. Fighter A throws lead jab

**Invitation Drill/Tactic 4
(Jamming and Hitting)**

4. ...which B counters with right crossing over A's left by timing the attack

5. ...and B uses left elbow to close the gap to close range jamming opponent's punches...

6. From this range B can shoulder stop to defend against punches

7. ...and to throw short inside punches

Rapid Assault Tactics
(Straight Blast Drill)

In this drill enter with a low kick (side, hook or foot jab) straight blast should be fast and explosive forcing your partner to peddle backwards off balance with his arms in front of his face. Excellent drill and effective tactic in all-out sparring to penetrate your partner's defense. In all-out fighting a rapid combination of elbows and knees would follow to knock the opponent out.

1. Both opponents face off

2. Fighter B closes the gap with low inside hook kick

3. ...and immediately throws straight right...

6. ...left straight blast

4. Left hand punch

7. ...right straight blast

5. ...changes to straight blast right

8. ...left straight blast

5 — ADVANCED JKD STRATEGIES

The growth and development of martial arts in the last decade of the 20th century was nothing less than phenomenal. This trend has continued into the 21st century. Fighters today possess more technical knowledge of different martial arts than was possible in an earlier era. Tactics and strategies have become a fighter's 'possessive' ingredient for success. Cross training is not only common, but expected in some quarters. Because today's fighter is versed in such a wide array of martial arts techniques that the term 'mixed martial arts' has been used to describe them.

Even more remarkable is that Bruce is now considered a cultural icon in the Chinese-speaking world. When he was alive, most Chinese Kung Fu masters resented this brash young man who was so openly dismissive of them and their methods. Bruce was capable of taking elements and concepts from other forms of fighting arts – traditional or non-traditional – and able to modify and integrate within his own framework. He said: "Jeet Kune Do favours form less so that it can assume all forms, and since it has no style, therefore Jeet Kune Do fits in with all styles…in this art, efficiency is anything that scores."

The student must be able to adapt to any situation and fit in with his opponent whether the opponent is a boxer or a wrestler etc. In the past (and many still do) martial arts instructors confined by their fighting principles taught their students to employ the same tactics regardless of the type of opponent you're fighting. No one fights the same way, strategies that work against one type of opponent may not work against another. It is up to the fighter to examine what strategies work for him which can be effectively applied against an opponent.

The tactics and strategies you use will be profoundly influenced by the type of opponent you encounter and the technique and tactics he employs. This is where your observational and analytical skills come into play, which can be enhanced through training with exponents from a wide array of backgrounds and styles. After you discover and analyze the adversary's strengths and weaknesses you'll be in a position to come up with a strategy to outwit him.

Some fighters will be punchers, some will be kickers, some will be grapplers. You need to be able to deal with all of these and flow among the different ranges and styles. Some opponents will be very analytical and studied in how they approach a fight. On the other hand you may encounter 'wild' men who crash in throwing everything at you in a frenzied flurry of punches, kicks and head butts like a savage street fighter.

Certain strategies will work best against certain types of opponents, and the more you know about your opponent the better your chances of fighting him more effectively. An empirical background on him will help you evaluate his tendencies, then you can attack his weaknesses whilst avoiding his strengths. A fighter basically can be split into two categories, the intelligent and mechanical fighter. The intelligent fighter will suss his opponent out before using any type of fighting strategy. Being able to sense your opponent's game plan requires observational skills – which is considered the highest level of fighting skill. A mechanical type of fighter is conditioned to fighting in a certain manner who will use repetitive attacks and pattern, and lacks the ability to experiment and analyse before attacking.

Of the vast amount of tactics in your arsenal, you should employ the ones that you are most familiar with which will surprise your opponent. The idea is to control your opponent and not vice versa. An effective strategy according to Bruce is to oppose the opposite tactics to those favoured by the adversary, ie box a wrestler, grapple a boxer. Another simple tactic to use against any type of opponent is to strike a vulnerable target, ie shin, groin, eye – to 'soften up' an assailant as a prelude to a grappling takedown or submission, or for that matter to enter close quarters for launching a barrage of quick and explosive headbutts, elbows and knees for total destruction.

Bruce was a combat strategies. He included techniques not only from Wing Chun into JKD but also other styles of Kung Fu, Karate, Judo, JuJitsu, Wrestling, Tang Sodgo, Western Boxing and Fencing. Tactics and strategies make up an imperative part and structure of Jeet Kune Do. As you will discover, these elements are crucial in defeating an opponent. The important principle in JKD is to learn to fit with any opponent or range at which you happen to be in when fighting. And employ the most effective tactics that will render the adversary helpless. Against someone with the same skill level or strength level as you, a sudden change of strategy or tactic can take him by full surprise and change the whole outcome of the bout.

VARIOUS TYPES OF OPPONENTS

Boxer: Bruce Lee felt that Western boxers were the hardest punchers. As can be seen from his notes on boxing. A boxer uses efficient footwork, a lot of defensive head and body movement, never static unlike traditional martial artists, ie karateka. A boxer is a very well conditioned athlete with a high level of attributes developed by intense hardcore training regime. On the other hand a boxer is restricted to fight the adversary in a certain manner. Although good at infighting (multi combinations in the clinch) he lacks close range grappling and on the ground he is helpless. Bobbing and weaving will make it difficult to hit (punch) the boxer, so low groin and knee kicks are very effective, because he is not used to defending these perimeters.

Thai Boxers: One of the most feared full contact sports is Thai Boxing. The kicking method of a Thai boxer advocates the philosophy of putting the bodyweight behind the kick and kick 'through' using the shin and instep. These fighters are dangerous in the kicking and the clinch range. Low round kicks to the legs can break the opponent's base and close range knees and elbows can be devastating to knocking out their opponent. To neutralize a kick boxer's strengths you will need to use various tactics, ie catch his kicking leg and completely off balance him or throw him to the ground. If you end up in the clinch it may be safer to look for a neck/head hold or lock; better still take him down before he can inflict any serious damage with his knees and elbows.

Grappler/Wrestler: This type of opponent is very dangerous in the close range. Wrestlers tend to be strong and generally big. A wrestler lacks striking ability but is the master of takedowns, pinning holds and physically conditioned. A jujitsu fighter is the master of the clinch who will try to take his opponent to the ground immediately. Master of the ground game as has been proved in NHB competitions. This type of opponent can injure himself in the street on the ground because many of the techniques are suitable for the mat as opposed to the hard ground in the street. When fighting a grappler, it is wise to keep your tactical options open. If you cannot finish the opponent with your striking skills you should be well versed in the grappling range yourself to increase your chances of survival in street fighting.

Savage Streetfighter: This type of fighter can come in several different packages, generally you want to find out what he's capable of. You are likely to encounter a streetfighter who has no formal training in an art, but his meanness and brute strength will be his greatest asset or attribute. Wild swings, head butts, and vicious language to go with it is common with streetfighters of this kind. Broken rhythm style grabbing, pulling, pushing with no real concern with real technique can even confuse the more experienced fighter/martial artist. Many a streetfighter's experience in the real world makes up for his lack of technique.

In the following pages you will discover tactics and strategies against different types of opponents. Although the five ways of attack developed by Bruce Lee are part of the

Jeet Kune Do strategies they have been covered in other books so I have not culminated on this aspect. May I stress that had Bruce lived I am sure he would have integrated much more elements into his Jeet Kune Do. It is up to us to take Bruce's original concepts and conglomerate them with modern concepts to make ourselves much more effective fighters!

Please note that this is by no means to demean the other fighting arts, rather I have illustrated how various JKD strategies can be applied against different types of opponents.

1. Larry faces a boxer

2. Boxer jabs which Larry inside parries simultaneously finger jabbing his eyes

3. As the boxer throws a wild right hook, Larry covers with left hand and palm strikes jaw...

Against a Boxer
(Bruce Lee's headlock)

a) An effective strategy against a fighterwho prefers long range punching is to jam him, ie crowd in close to prevent him from throwing his long punches

b) A good strategy against a counterpunching, defensive type of fighter is to continue to push him with aggressive combinations

c) Knappling techniques can also be used to counter punching against a boxer

d) Low, rapid kicks and double/single leg tackles are very effective tactics against a boxer

4. Then shoulder stops and traps boxer's arm simultaneously left punching face

5. Larry quickly grabs the neck for control

6. ...twisting him down, striking with downward elbow to the face

7. …then wrapping arm around neck into head lock

1. Larry faces off with a boxer

2. Larry catches the jab with the right hand and throws a finger jab...

3. The boxer tries to set up hook/uppercut

Against a Boxer

4. Larry checks the boxer's right hand while wrapping neck...

5. ...quickly wraps neck and pivots to outside twisting opponent down...

6. ...and follows up with right kn ee to head. From here Larry can knock out with multiple knees

1. Boxer and Larry face off

2. Larry slips inside boxer's jab and gets on the inside

3. As the boxer throws uppercut, Larry catches the elbow. (Larry could headbutt from this position)...

Against a Boxer
(Bruce Lee's Neck Crank)

4. ...Larry throws right palm to face whilst holding boxer's right elbow...

5. ...and steps around while cranking on the boxer's neck...

6. ...Larry puts pressure on the neck to send the boxer to sleep

ADVANCED JKD STRATEGIES

1. Once again Larry faces a boxer

2. Larry puts down the boxer's low jab

3. As the Boxer crosses Larry catches punch and intercepts with a straight kick to the stomach...

Against a Boxer

4. As foot lands, Larry traps the boxer's foot while shifting his balance spirally and hits left palm to groin…

5. From here Larry, while monitoringthe boxer's lead hand, pushes him off balance while shoving on the face

1. Larry and boxer face off

2. Larry parries the cross

3. ...and bobs down under boxer's hook

4. ...moving behind him sneaks in left uppercut to ribs...

7. ...as the boxer falls Larry palms his face

8. ...controls the arm

Against a Boxer
(Bruce Lee's Arm Lock)

5. Coming up from behind popping his chest and shoulders

6. ...and steps back pulling

9. ...steps over...

10. ...sits back into an armlock

1. Larry faces a Thai/kick boxer

2. Kick boxer does switch step to set up round kick...

3. Larry catches kick and wraps leg

a) With the popularity of Muay Thai, it is not unusual to encounter a fighter who is proficient with the Thai round kick. Stay at a distance – let him take the initiative then counter attack

b) Once again single leg/double leg pick-ups, sweeps and trips are all effective tactics against a Thai/kick boxer

c) If you end up in the clinch pay close attention to your opponent's knees and elbows. Try to go for an immediate throw – use head butts, hair pulling, pinching and open hand (palm smash) if necessary

d) Always try to catch the opponent's kicking leg – this will put you in an advantage position – where you can strike and take down

Against a Kick/Thai Boxer
(Bruce Lee's Leg Catch and Trip)

4. Then strikes with left palm or finger jab...

5. ...kicks supporting leg...

6. ...and does leg sweep...

7. Takes opponent down and locks the leg and strike him with the left hand

7b. ...to take one step further Larry can turn his opponent and apply a reverse leg lock for even total control

1. Larry and kick boxer face off

2. Opponent attacks with righgt knee strike which Larry uses right elbow and arm to stop

3. ...and sweeps opponent's leg and arm inside...

Against a Kick/Thai Boxer

4. ...and strikes with a hard right elbow to the face...

5. ...then quickly steps behind locking neck and pulls back and down...

6. ...as the opponent falls, Larry wrist locks while stomp kicking to the head

1. Larry faces his opponent

2. Kick boxer initiates a round/side kick...

3....which Larry sweeps aside with right parry...

Against a Kick/Thai Boxer
(Bruce Lee's Evade and Attack)

4. ...as soon as the opponent faces his back in an off balance position, Larry is in a perfect position to throw a right hook kick to the inside leg – alternatively he can kick the groin

1. Larry on right JKD onguard stance. His opponent in left stance

2. Opponent starts front kick...

5. ...and front kicks the opponent's groin...

6. ...then pivots to the right

ADVANCED JKD STRATEGIES

Against a Kick/Thai Boxer
(Bruce Lee's Leg Catch and Forward Trip and Lock)

3. Larry catches the opponent's kick

4. ...pushing him off balance

7. ...taking down the opponent by left leg trip and pushing him off balance...

8. ...then steps over into single leg lock

1. The wrestler squats down to tackle Larry

2. As soon as the wrestler gets in range to tackle, Larry sidesteps, twisting his head

3. ...continues pivoting

a) Against a grappler you must keep your strategy options open. You can defeat a grappler with pounding him with heavy blows or out-grapple him if you yourself are proficient in grappling

b) If you feel you're insecure in close range, stay at a distance and work on 'neutralising strategy' (finger jab to eyes to kicking the groin)

c) If you end up in the clinch or on the floor, use y our striking tools in conjunction with grappling techniques to inflict pain on the opponent

d) Learn to 'push off' the opponent and strike with the legs in rapid style fashion for knocking out someone who is trying to clinch or shoot for leg tackle

Against a Wrestler

4. ...and knees the wrestler in head while maintaining kneck control...

5. ...Larry drops to left knee, locking opponent's neck...

6. ...twisting him around...

7. Larry uses body to forward neck crank

1. Wrestler attempts to tackle/clinch Larry…

2. Larry wraps his arm around the opponent while maintaning balance

3. …and drops to left knee dragging opponent down…

Against a Wrestler

4. ...rolling him onto back...

5. ...locks opponent into quarter stock position

1. Larry and wrestler face off

4. ...opponent tries for a right headlock, Larry pops up his arm...

2. Both fighters end up in close range clinch position

5. ...then moves behind opponent locking his hips...

3. Larry shifts to the right

6. ...dropping to one knee and traps opponent's left foot

Against a Wrestler
(Takedown to Bruce Lee's side headlock)

7. ...and pulls down opponent using right arm...

8. ...rapidly mounting and head butting simultaneously

9a. ...finishes with a guillotine hold

9b. Alternatively finish 'Two' would be Bruce Lee's headlock

1. Larry and grappler struggle and grapple with each other

2. ...Larry's opponent steps in for a hip throw

Against a Wrestler

3. ...Larry wraps his left arm around and bases himself by putting all his weight down to stall the throw, at the same time Larry head butts his opponent

1. Larry and wrestler ready for attack in close range

2. Larry's opponent moves into am arm drag throw by grabbing Larry's arm

3. ...Larry checks opponent's hip with right hand as left arm hooks over his right arm

Against a Wrestler

4. ... Larry drops to knee pulling down on opponent's neck...

5. ...pulling him down and rolling into...

6. ...an overarm triangle neck lock left knee to the face...

!. Larry faces the streetfighter, who...

2. ...grabs and brings his right fist up telegraphing a punch...

a) You never know what you're going to encounter in a street fight. You need to be prepared for anything. The best defence is offence – as soon as you think the opponent is going to attack, intercept him.

b) After countering always follow up and press your advantage forcing the opponent to b e on the defensive or forcing him down.

c) Be aware of wild swings and broken rhythm style attacks from the streetfighter.

d) Use techniques and tactics that will surprise the streetfighter and leave him in a helpless position. When the opponent is on the ground continue to strike with your foot.

Against a savage Streetfighter

3. Larry covers the punch with his left elbow

4. ...and wraps arm with overarm hook and palm strike to face

5, ...then puts pressure on the elbow joint to exert sheer pain for total control which has the streetfighter crying for mercy

1. Larry and the streetfighter face off. Streetfighter seems aggressive...

2. ...then brings his right hand back to throw wide hook

3. ...which Larry slips and intercepts with a right hook...

Against a Savage Streetfighter

4. ...and knees opponent's groin

5. ...then locks neck pulling opponent down...

6. ...and forward

7. ...and knees to the buttocks to finish him off

Against a Savage Streetfighter

1. Streetfighter grabs Larry

2. Larry pins left hand

3. Opponent throws right punch which Larry parries

6. ...wrapping neck while maintaining split finger lock

4. ...bends opponent's wrist down into

7. ...and taking him down

5. ...split finger lock...

8. ...and tightens lock with both hands

1. Larry and streetfighter face off

2. Streetfighter fires rapid wild forward pressure punches

Against a Savage Streetfighter

3. ...Larry parries left cross...

4. ...and sidesteps

5. ...fut sao upward under armpit...

6. ...and breaking the opponent's kneecap with a low jeet tek kick

APPENDIX

BRUCE LEE'S ENERGY DRILLS

Q – WHAT ATTRIBUTES ARE DEVELOPED PRACTICING ENERGY DRILLS AND HOW WILL THESE QUALITIES AID ME IN REAL COMBAT.

A – Energy Drills are unique method of training for developing certain skills and honing a number of crucial qualities that are essential. Its important to remember Energy Drills are a means to an end not an end in itself, in other words it's a method to enhance your reaction time, your linear procedure, sensitivity in the arms, timing and the ability to 'read' the opponents energy so you can feel instantly if he is putting hard or soft pressure, forward, pulling, upwards or downwards or sideways pressure. Through Prolonged repetitious drilling the student will yield mechanical precision and sharpness in his technique.

Q – MOST OF THE TIME I HAVE FOR TRAINING I DEDICATE TO REALISTIC APPLICATIONS AND CONTACT SPARRING, I WOULD LIKE TO INCORPORATE ONLY SOME OF THE MOST PRACTICAL ENERGY DRILLS INTO MY SCHEDULE WHICH WILL ENHANCE MY SENSITIVITY FROM A PRACTICAL POINT OF VIEW, WHICH DRILLS WOULD YOU RECOMMEND FOR ME.

A – The word in itself 'sensitivity' could mean several different aspects of your personal interaction with the martial arts. To make the training much more combative I recommend you perform, lets say, lopsau to lopsau drill or chi sau and add in arm locks, arm bars and even go for a neck trap when you feel or see an opening. You could step outside of the circumference and train the grappling range 'neck trapping 'drills (as seen in my book 'Jeet Kune Do Conditioning and Grappling Methods) which develop sensitivity in a more combative manner. Of course, in JKD drills should be practiced in a manner closely approximating the way the skill will be executed in actual combat.

Q – CAN CHI SAU – AN INTEGRAL EXERCISE OF BRUCE LEE'S JEET KUNE DO – BE EXPERIENCED BY EXPERIMENTING ON MY OWN WITH A PARTNER OR IS IT IMPERATIVE TO TRAIN WITH SOMEONE COGNIZANT.

A – OK in chi sau you need someone with experience in doing chi sau properly or an instructor so that he can teach you the proper concept and energy to use. This exercise requires both partners to roll their arms in a harmonious manner. Its important you learn and apply the important little tips on performing this exercise correctly to derive the necessary benefits it offers. The ultimate level being the ability to react instantly with total mind and body coordinated to fit in with the opponents movements and energy.

Q – I AM RATHER SMALL IN STATURE AND FIND IT HARD TO
OVERPOWER A BIGGER STRONGER PARTNER WHEN TRAINING, HOW CAN I USE HIS ENERGY AGAINST HIM.

A – First of all if you are small in stature and find it hard to overpower a training partner while performing energy drills, its important you learn to use his strength against him. In other words redirect his attacks or oncoming pressure or force, relax and learn to make use of sensitivity by being quick and fast as soon as you feel pressure in a certain direction. If he's applying pushing force direct towards you do not apply pressure forward towards him, rather pull him towards you off balance him. A smaller person can make up for his small size by applying the Chinese philosophy of 'being soft yet not giving in' and by applying minimum effort to gain the most in a more efficient manner rather than brute force which can actually make you stiff and inflexible in motion.

Q – WHEN CAN I FREE-SPAR IN CHI SAU.

A – Once you have the basic concept and can efficiently roll your arms in a smooth flowing manner with a partner, and can apply single techniques whilst practicing chi sau, you can start free-sparring. It is al so suggested that you eliminate all jerky and errors movements and concentrate on getting the technique right at this stage.

Q – WHEN CAN I ADVANCE TO BLINDFOLD CHI SAU.

A – Blind fold chi sau can be done by just closing your eyes, its not necessary to put a blindfold on. Bruce used to do this exercise to show his chi sau skills by using a blindfold. He was a true master at this exercise. This would be your last stage, you have to have the proper trapping, proper sensitivity and energy and a high level of tactile awareness before advancing to this level. This stage requires the student to be able to feel the right energy instantly without seeing it coming and redirecting it with the right counter at the right time.

JKD TRAPPING

Q – HOW IS JEET KUNE DO TRAPPING MODIFIED FROM WING CHUN.

A – Bruce Lee started to develop his own system of jeet kune do by modifying different ranges. He began to expound on various elements which he thought were useful to him and modifying what he thought could be made much more better in terms of functionality. He modified the stance and made it much more mobile and would add various attack elements to get into the trapping structure. So he would begin from the out of range and flow from trapping to grappling smoothly. Bruce began to emphasize hitting and trapping only if the line of attack became obstructed, so compound trapping counter for counter as seen in wing chun was modified to an certain extent for directness purposes.

Q – WHERE SHOULD I PUT MY LEAD FOOT WHEN TRAPPING UP MY OPPONENT.
A – Personally myself I prefer to step on the adversary's foot, this will trap his lead foot and he will not be able to kick you in the groin, also this will not allow him to move back as you dispense and unload a barrage of punches or as you apply a head or neck hold after you've successfully trapped up his arms. So this simple yet often neglected concept should be employed in the trapping range to give you an edge and to avoid being kicked when trapping.

Q – WHERE DO I PAK THE OPPONENTS ARM, WRIST, FOREARM OR NEAR THE ELBOW.

A – You can do all the above. Some people like to pak on the wrist, some forearm, some on the elbow. It also depends what distance you're at when you pak the opponents arm. The disadvantage of paking the wrist is that he may be able to release and easily counter. If you pak on the forearm or near the elbow area and put enough forward pressure simultaneously hit with the lead hand to the face, it will make it harder for him to release himself.

Q – WHEN TRAPPING UP MY PARTNERS ARM(S) HE SEEMS TO ALWAYS EASILY DISENGAGE AND RELEASE, WHAT AM I DOING WRONG.

A – If he easily disengages you, you're not putting enough forward pressure and really trapping his arm into his body. Bruce lee used to really push the arm all the way into his opponents body where its very hard to release it and disengage to go to a counter throwing a jau sau. You need to time it right and be very quick about it or the partner will just simply step away or kick you. There are many counters to pak sau, so its important you develop the right technique in trapping this is where 'practice makes perfect' comes into play.

Q – WHAT IS THE PURPOSE OF PRACTICING COMPOUND TRAPPING WITH A COOPERATIVE PARTNER FROM REFERENCE POINT BECAUSE NO ONE REALLY FIGHTS LIKE THIS IN THE STREET.

A – Bruce used to say 'you start within the nucleus which is from the reference point, back out of the nucleus where you're not touching hands, then back in to the nucleus' reference point trapping practice is just a progression, its like you cannot go to D before you go through A, B and C, this way you learn and apply the correct mechanics and technique which is important before you flow from trap to trap until you develop each tool into an 'art'. Trapping is a means to an end not an end in itself in jeet kune do. Bruce later on broke away from the idea of trapping for the sake of trapping, the ultimate concept hear was to hit the opponent and only trap if you're line of attack is obstructed or blocked by the opponent. The reason for training trapping in compound trapping combinations is to develop the combative and mechanical qualities and technique so you learn to counter to counter. In real combat you I profess you trap and attack hard and fast so your opponent does not even get a chance to block your second hit. In the street your opponent will not give you the structure or response that of your cooperative training partner in the classroom environment.

Q – AGAINST A BOXER OR SOMEONE WITH A VERY CLOSE GUARD DOES TRAPPING REALLY WORK AND HOW DO I GAIN AN ATTACHMENT.

A – You can gain an attachment by just waiting, timing the opponents lead hand punch or jab or the rearhand. Western Boxers tight guard and lightning fast punches from all angles makes it much more difficult to trap. Once you attach and clash or end in a clinch position you need to trap with speed. i would also recommend trying to press capture his jab – to parry it then go in – or initiate by throwing 'garbage' to gain an attachment. A boxers defensive guard and structure makes it hard but trapping can be employed if done correctly, just like anything else there are ways to succeed if the methods and tactics are performed properly with the right timing and speed.

Q – WHAT IS THE "NPM PRINCIPLE" (NO PASSIVE MOVES) OR THE JKD'S THIRD HAND IN JKD TRAPPING.

A – Actually the No Passive Moves is what I term 'you hit first then trap and hit instead of trap then hit or trap trap and hit. In other words you're hitting on the second beat before you trap before firing in a extra shot in between and this is where the speed and fluidity comes into play. You're constantly hitting, that's the main concept and trapping can be secondary sometimes or primarily either way. Bruce was so fast at performing this trapping principle that it was hard for the observer to distinguish and be able to detect the extra punch that Bruce would sneak in between. This again verifies that the principle idea in jeet kune do is to hit and trap if required in opposed to looking for a trap.

Q – WHAT COMMON FOLLOW UPS DO YOU RECOMMEND AFTER TRAPPING BOTH OF THE ADVERSARY'S ARMS.

A – The common follow ups I would recommend after trapping up would be short range punching, shovel hook, uppercut, hooking, straight blast, also very effective tactics would be devastating headbutts, elbows and knees at this range. There are many ways to follow up sometimes its according to the opponent s position after you tie up one or two arms. Locking to takedowns into submission is effective follow up. The idea is to go with the flow, if you're good with your hands you might want to hit if you're a good grappler you may want to flow immediately into the grappling mode. The beauty of being able to tie up both of the adversary's arms leaves him almost helpless and you in a position to attack hard and fast without any obstruction.

Q – HOW DID BRUCE MAKE USE OF TRAPPING IN SPARRING AND HOW CAN TRAPPING BE IMPLEMENTED IN A SPARRING MODE.

A – First of all you have to cover the basic two ranges in sparring to get into the trapping range – this would be you're kicking and punching ranges – But these can be closed very quickly if for example you close the gap by hitting a low line shin or round kick and flow into a pak sau and punch to the face, or if he initiates with a jab which you can double hand parry the jab and trap and hit. This requires a lot of good timing and a lot of practice so it's a good idea to use boxing gloves or fingerless gloves which are commonly available today and set up your trapping by using footwork distance and timing. Bruce could intercept an oncoming kick, destroy the lead leg and shift into trap and hit smoothly. He would also use different entrys with low line kicks to get into the trapping range, of course his main objective was to hit and not look for a trap, and trap only when his line of attack was obstructed by the opponent's block etc.

JKD WOODEN DUMMY TRAINING

Q – WHICH QUALITIES ARE TRAINED BY USING THE WOODEN DUMMY.

A – Wooden Dummy is an invaluable training apparatus in jeet kune do which builds speed, timing, simultaneous strike and block, 4 corner defense, your linear, coordination and explosiveness in movement and body shifting. The more you practice the better skillful you'll become and increase your sharpness. A lot of short quick bursts of explosive and fast combinations can be developed to increase all the above qualities.

Q – WHAT ADVICE WOULD YOU GIVE TO SOMEONE JUST STARTING OFF TO TRAIN ON THE DUMMY.

A – I would advice you to find somebody who could teach you very well, personally I would find somebody who really knew the movements and show you what each movement on the dummy would relate to an actual person. Bruce Lee had 57 wooden Dummy movements in the JKD set before he passed away which should be learned to give you a base and understanding, then you can advance to free flowing techniques in later stages.

Q – SHOULD I PURCHASE A DUMMY WITH A EXTENDED LEG LIKE BRUCE LEE'S DUMMY
A – Yes, I would try to purchase a dummy with a extended leg so you can practice your low line kicking. This also allows you to put your lead leg next to the Dummy's leg so the opponent will find it hard to throw a kick when you're in the trapping range.

Q – DID BRUCE LEE USE THE DUMMY IN A MORE FREESTYLE MANNER AND HOW DID HE MODIFY THE TECHNIQUES FROM THE CLASSICAL METHOD OF TRAINING.

A – Bruce would take the classical systems and take it out of context and free express himself on the Dummy. He would treat the Dummy as a opponent and would punch, kick, stick trap, and move like he was fighting an opponent. He could move in and out unloading blindingly fast movements that was like listening to a machine gun firing. Although the dummy could not hit back unlike an sparring partner it was very useful for training when one has no access to a partner.

Q – I FEEL ONCE I GET STUCK IN WORKING OUT ON THE DUMMY MY SPEED EXPLOSIVENESS ETC ARE PROFOUNDLY TAKEN TO A WHOLE NEW LEVEL FEELING GREAT AND PSYCHED UP, JUST HOW MUCH TIME SHOULD BE SET ASIDE FOR TRAINING ON THIS UNIQUE PIECE OF EQUIPMENT.

A – That would be up to the individual and the level of skill they are in pursuit of attaining and developing pertaining to the Dummy. Some people put in just enough time to maintain their sharpness and technique so they don't forget the moves. Others can put in a larger percentage of their training schedule with the aim of reaching a certain level or to accelerate their performance. This is a hard question to answer for everybody because every one is different. All in all, I would say even 20 minutes of three times a week Dummy training will keep you sharp and maintain your maximum level.

Q – DO YOU RECOMMEND WALL BAGS TO BE STUCK ON WHICH ARE COMMONLY AVAILABLE NOWADAYS OR HITTING SOLID WOOD IS BETTER FOR HARDENING THE HAND.

A – Sigung Bruce Lee used a sand wall bag stuck on the wall. Today you can purchase wall bags which can be stuck on the dummy so you can hit with full power when working with the Dummy, but even if you don't have these, you will still condition your fists, arms, wrists palms and elbows, because you can use contact on the wood to a certain degree which will condition your body without risking injury.

JKD SPARRING

Q – WHAT KIND OF GLOVES SHOULD BE WORN WHEN DRILLING AND SPARRING. I FEEL BIG BULKY GLOVES TEND TO SLOW ME DOWN AND LIGHT GLOVES HAVE LESS PROTECTION.

A – When I was sparring back in the seventies, we used to wear 16oz gloves for conditioning of the arm, that's a pound on each hand. But also I would recommend experimenting with 14oz and 12oz gloves. There are some gloves on the market which may seem light but offer very little protection in the wrist area and in terms of taking a hard punch there's very little padding.

Q – WHAT ADVICE WOULD YOU GIVE TO A BEGINNER WHO WANTS TO BEGIN SPARRING.
A – First one would be technical, plus the conditioning definitely, ninety percent is conditioning before you spar. I'd have a check up with a doctor to see if you have any problems. There's an old saying "when all is equal strength will tell" so the conditioning is number one aspect before sparring, in any contact sport. Most importantly start off slowly and progress as soon as you acclimatise yourself to full contact. Do not be thrown

into the deep end right away, but work your way up, or else you may not want to continue this type of training which is a very important element in a martial artists training program.

Q – WHAT HEADGEAR IS APPROPRIATE FOR SPARRING, IT TENDS TO HAVE EFFECT ON MY VISION WHEN SPARRING.

A – I recommend what fits you personally, there are many different types of headgear out there from ringside, title etc, leather headguard is much better than wearing a vinyl type which many semi contact people tend to use. When I used to spar I always tried to get one which doesn't slip around your head when you get hit, Buy one that fits tight and secure also which doesn't mess up your peripheral vision.

Q – WHEN SPARRING I ALWAYS TEND TO GET HIT WITH A BARRAGE OF PUNCHES, BUT I WANT TO EXPERIENCE FULL CONTACT SPARRING IN A HIGH PRESSURE ENVIRONMENT WITH A NON COOPERATIVE PARTNER TO ELIMINATE MY FEARS OF GETTING HIT.

A – A good trainer will not put you in the ring with a professional fighter whose going to use you for meat. What happens is you get 'gun shy', in other words when your partner returns the punches you flinch and be just like a moving heavy bag. The major factor here is to work your technical with a good sparring partner and have a good trainer above all and progress from there. Sparring lightly in the beginning will pave the way for heavier intensive rounds once you have a sound knowledge and experience of taking and dishing out punishment. Sparring full contact can and will affect your mental and psychological side, its important to get into the water to get a real feel of swimming, Sparring must be experienced to get as close to reality as possible and to psychologically be prepared.

Q – MY PARTNER SEEMS TO BE EVERY WHERE, NEVER STILL AND HIS TIMING GUARD AND DISTANCE IS ALWAYS RIGHT, HOW CAN I INSTILL ALL THESE QUALITIES IN MY OWN MOVEMENTS.

A – Practice, practice and more practice. Drilling is the backbone of developing mechanical precision in technique and movement. Practice sparring drills with a partner by moving around who is also moving and hitting back instead of standing there like a immovable robot. This way you'll learn to fight in motion and be able to relate to the opponents movement. So its essential you practice this way to instill the necessary qualities which will aid you in your sparring sessions.

Q – HOW DO I DEVELOP THE RIGHT "ATTITUDE" IN SPARRING.

A – My attitude is you get what you give and take what you give, in other words try to be cool under the harshness of circumstances and try never to show pain if you're hurt. Throw away the ego before you enter the training session and psych your self up mentally. Sparring is not a contest but a means to experience full contact with a non cooperative partner and learn not only to hit, avoid being hit and move around, but to be able to take punishment in a safe environment. Attitude is what sets apart the professional from the novice. Its important to have the right attitude in training and respect for your training partners.

Q – SHOULD ONE START OFF WITH 75 PERCENT CONTACT BEFORE GOING FULL CONTACT ROUNDS TO AVOID SERIOUS INJURY.

A – I think when sparring full contact you should have the protective gear such as the cup, mouth piece, headgear. You should make the sparring between light, medium and may be some hard sparring as you advance along and as your conditioning and technical prowess increases.

Q – WHAT ARE THE "JKD'S RAPID ASSAULT TACTICS" AND HOW CAN THEY BE DRILLED WITH PROTECTIVE GEAR.

A – What I assume this means is you beat your opponent to the punch or kick and to integrate what I call progressive indirect attack you might fake to one area to get to another area to soften the opponent, then finish him with a rapid multiple straight blasts or other fast explosive combination to totally take him out by surprise. The idea is to enter or intercept with a hit to a preferably vulnerable target to inject pain, whilst the opponent is in agony you immediately launch your rapid assault attacks.

Q – HOW DO I BREAK MY OPPONENT'S RHYTHM.

A – There's an old saying "you never punch with a puncher, you never kick with a kicker, you never box with a boxer". To break an opponent's rhythm you can employ several methods. A sudden halt in between exchanging a combination of blows, a sudden change of tactic by exploding into the opponent's defence ie rapid assault attacks, compound feints before attacking to confuse and cause him to 'un-set', increase or decrease the cadence to offset his timing, and a sudden change of tactic completely ie, from punching to exploding into grappling. These are some of the ways you can break the adversary's rhythm.

Q – WHICH FEINTS AND FAKES WORK EFFECTIVELY IN SPARRING.

A – It's the ones you work on, no two people are the same or fight the same way. As you advance and spar more you'll find little things that work for you, it all comes down to experimentation and your adversary's reaction. some people are very good with faking with their eyes that can throw the adversary off and redirect his attention. Head and shoulder fakes are good close range fakes. One of the best ways to practice feinting is in front of a full-length mirror which requires imagination and visualization. Generally, work on a diverse range of feints in sparring that tend to take your partner by surprise or has him react the way you want him to react.

Q – HOW DO I LURE (USING ABD) MY OPPONENT IN TO A TRAP AND SUDDENLY OVERWHELM HIM.

A – Sometimes you can lure your opponent into a trap by giving the impression that you're hurt or out of 'gas' (tired) or by dropping your guard either lead or rear hand or both hands to make him attack you. Once he initiates the attack you may counterattack, this requires precise timing and a high level of skill.

Q – JKD IS BASED ON FOUR RANGES OF COMBAT, HOW DOES ONE DEVELOP COMPETENT IN ALL FOUR AREAS TO A SATISFACTORY LEVEL.

A – Based on the four ranges of combat, the best way you can develop your skills to an optimum level is to train with different people who specialise in each range, in other words cross-train. The modern martial artist must defy the old stereotypes and act as a melting pot for any particular system and techniques. A good grappler might help you with your grappling but might not be versed in hitting so you might want to find someone who is primarily a striker, now, this striker may not be cognizant in the trapping range so you should find some body with a maybe wing chun background for trapping. This is not to say you need a special instructor for each range, it's possible to develop a high standard with one coach, more and more people are cross training and are cognizant in different ranges of combat. Secondly, it will depend on the amount of time you are willing to dedicate and expend to training any one of these facets, so it really depends on the individual. To go one step further, a person might spend a large chunk of his training time dedicated to developing one range ie grappling because this may be his stronger range and the remaining portion of the time available training his punching and kicking etc. Bruce was advocating cross training long before it became the in-thing, at that time cross training was violently opposed. Today cross training is 'the thing' and accepted openly in the martial arts circles. Cross training does not mean you have to go and learn 5 different arts, the underlying factor is that the jkd student is strong in all four ranges of combat.

Q – WHAT GEAR WAS USED IN THE LA CHINATOWN SCHOOL AND HOW DID THE STUDENTS SPAR.

A – Back in the Chinatown days we did not have the benefits of the shinguards and the body armour that we have access to today. So we used kendo body armour, the baseball shinguards. the old navy headgear with the bar and the 14oz boxing gloves or the fingerless kendo gloves (as seen in Enter The Dragon) and the cup, and mouth piece. The sparring was full contact, a lot of low line side kicks, side kick to intercept which was really based on timing and accuracy. The sparring also based on physical conditioning and once you took off the gear and armour you really felt light. The drills and sparring rounds were perceived as closer to realty as possible and directed to street survival skills rather than sport fighting or boxing.

ADVANCED JEET KUNE DO STRATEGIES

Q – BOXERS TEND TO HAVE FAST POWERFUL HANDS, WHAT IS THE SECRET TO AVOID BEING HIT AND KEEPING HIM AT DISTANCE.

A – First you should train your defensive posture, such as your slipping moving your head, train your reaction drills against a boxer, working with the speed ball to develop eye hand coordination, footwork using distance as an advantage rather than blocking. The secret is to disturb his lower section 'the leg' by intercepting his jabs with the jkd low side kick to his knee cap or kicking the groin area or stomach. Try to avoid clinching in punching range and use low rapid kicks if he advances.

Q – BRUCE LEE SAID BOX A WRESTLER, WRESTLE A BOXER, WHAT DID HE MEAN.

A – What Bruce meant by this was 'never do what your opponent expects or is a master of' in other words never kick with a kicker, never box with a boxer, never grapple with a grappler. The crucial concept here is to use tactics that your opponent is unfamiliar with and don't fall into his mode. This will not only help you score on him more effectively but will take him by complete surprise both physically and psychologically.

Q – WHAT TACTICS ARE EFFECTIVE IN AVOIDING A CLINCH FROM A GRAPPLER.
A – Footwork and distance is of prime importance. As he shoots in or tries for a clinch you can use one or both hands pushing him off whilst circling and fire in a combination of front lift kicks to the groin and stomach areas. This is a good strategy to avoid a tackle or clinch.

Q – WHAT STRATEGIES WORK AGAINST A SAVAGE STREETFIGHTER WITH NO FEAR AND WHO IS UNPREDICTABLE.

A – Use whatever is necessary. One of the crucial elements in dealing with this type of opponent is to control your adrenaline and use your killer instinct. Don't let his raw attitude break your psychological defence and confidence. Maintain your cool at all times and attack hard and fast directed to his vulnerable targets so he is no longer in position to maintain his attacks. You will find that the streetfighter or novice's rhythm will be hard to gauge because his attacks and movements are likely to be thrown – unintentionally – in a broken rhythm manner, which can easily fool even a experienced martial artist.

Q – CAN JEET KUNE DO TRAPPING BE USED ON THE GROUND AGAINST A GROUND-FIGHTER.

A – Yes. Especially in the mount position you can trap and hit. Also you can use it from the ground position scissors position, especially when the person's reaching to grab you, you can easily and effectively employ pak da inside pak and hit. You can tie up both of the opponents arms from the mount position leaving you the opportunity to strike him in the face. If the opponent has you in the double hand neck grab in the guard position, you can easily trap both his arms and hit a finger jab with the free hand. JKD philosophy advocates and emphasises adaptability and modification depending on the situation or position you happen to be in at any particular time. So jkd trapping on the ground can quite simply be very useful.

Q – WHAT ARE THE PRIME ELEMENTS THAT MAKE JEET KUNE DO'S INTERCEPTION ATTACKS SO EFFECTIVE.

A – It's based on the amount of training one puts into timing and distance drills, and this is one of the core reasons that makes it effective. On the other hand JKD employs direct defence – Attack strategy as opposed to defending then countering as seen in many other arts. In other words when my opponent throws a lead front kick, I will defend by stopping him by throwing a lead low side kick targeted to the oncoming kick, so I am defending and attacking – thus inflicting damage to my opponent – simultaneously with one single stroke. Bruce Lee was a master at intercepting, he could 'feel' what his opponent was going to do even before he launched an attack. The idea is to attack the opponent in midstream of his own attack, because he will be concentrating in his attack rather than his defense.

Q – HOW DO I TAKEDOWN A BOXER WHO KEEPS YOU AT BAY WITH HIS LIGHTNING LEAD JABS.

A – First of all if he is quick and fast don't try to chase him around but let him come to you. Once he is in range you can quickly shoot in with a double or single leg takedown. However if he keeps his distance you can employ the jkd's closing the distance strategy by entering with a low side or hook kick to the knee or shin cap area, this will inflict sudden pain allowing you to clinch or takedown with double or single leg takedown.

Q – WHAT IS A HIT-AND-RUN TYPE FIGHTER.

A – These type of fighters are very difficult because they like to move in quickly and hit maybe 4, 5 combination punches and quickly move out instantly. This fighter makes use of footwork and distance and avoids getting tied up, speed is another essential factor that plays a role within this fighters framework. Basically hit-and-run strategy is effective tactic which can be mastered through sparring.

Q – WHAT STRATEGIES ARE EFFECTIVE AGAINST TALL FIGHTER.

A – Against a tall fighter you may find it difficult to reach and he will have the advantage of reach over you. A relatively effective strategy is to get in on the inside and unleash heavy punishing blows to the stomach and rib areas to bring his guard down. This will put you in a position to use your overhand and uppercuts as he is bending down or transition into head or neck lock. Tall fighters tend to be slower.

Q – WHAT STRATEGIES ARE EFFECTIVE AGAINST A SMALL FIGHTER.

A – Fighting against a small fighter may not be easy as it looks. A small fighter may be quicker than you if you're much heavier. A good tactic to employ is to wait for him to come-in once he is in you can unload your combinations offsetting him completely. The vital point is to be prepared for any quick bursts of infighting attacks (Mike Tyson peeka-boo method) which are common with small smart fighters generally speaking or any other tricky manoeuvre which he may try to provoke you. A smaller fighter will try to attack closer targets to make up for his shorter reach.

Q – WHAT STRATEGIES ARE EFFECTIVE AGAINST A FAST FIGHTER.

A – I wouldn't try to match punch with punch. Rather use different tactics to slow him down or better still 'rush him' with a explosive clinch immobilising his hitting ability or crush his tools (hit him on the arms ie bicep or shoulder to slow his jab) or punches, kick him in the thigh or knee cap to inflict pain which will temporarily disable him. Hit hard and fast.

Q – WHAT STRATEGIES ARE EFFECTIVE AGAINST A SLOW FIGHTER.

A – A lot of quick combinations use him like a heavy bag go with the flow. If he is a Big slow fighter, he may be 250 pounds you may want to avoid clinching, instead use speedy attacks in and out.

Q – HOW DOES ONE CULTIVATE "KILLER INSTINCT".

A – Yes, killer instinct is an essential ingredient in a fighters arsenal which should be developed and honed through sparring and training in real life type scenarios. Bruce Lee advocated emotional content and intensity in his work outs, he believed each movement punch or kick you deliver should have this emotional element so you would develop the right mind frame in training which you would tap-in to yourself in actual combat. this killer instinct then becomes the psychological energy which pushes you in the fight. Every human being has killer instinct in him, the degree to which he can take it will vary from individual to individual. The trick is to be able to click on and off your killer instinct at will. The ability to do so requires you to have confidence and control over your emotional state. So how does one develop this state of mind which seems to be a crucial ingredient in fighting. Some people are aggressive in nature whilst some are more laid back, one needs to develop the right attitude and personality in combat. The bottom line being the need to insert emotional content in all aspect of your training wether you're hitting the Bag or pads or fighting grappling with a partner, the ability to master your mind and know yourself will give you a deeper understanding of combat.

Q – WHAT ROLE DO FOUL TACTICS – BITING, PINCHING, HAIR-PULLING – PLAY IN JEET KUNE DO.

A – Bruce had several of these which he did out of trapping range. But biting I would not recommend today because of the different diseases you can catch. Pinching is crucial to create an opening and for release. The hair-pulling to pull the opponent to take him off you or to surprise him instantly. These foul tactics are what I call desperation moves and Bruce lee integrate into his jeet kune do tools because of the effectiveness and are easily applicable regardless of your strength or size.

Q – TWO FIGHTERS WITH THE SAME LEVEL OF SKILL, WHAT SUDDEN CHANGE OF STRATEGY CAN CHANGE THE WHOLE FIGHT.

A – Usually when two fighters with the same level of skill are fighting, The one who is in better condition will have the edge. But there are certain 'sudden' strategies if employed can change the situation and break your opponents rhythm taking him by surprise. If both fighters have the same level of physical attributes the one with intellectual superiority will have an edge. On the other hand if the fighters are equally intelligent, then the one with superior technical and mechanical knowledge is likely to have an edge.

Q – HOW DO I TAKE OUT A KICKERS STRENGTH (ENVIRONMENT) SO HE IS IN NO POSITION TO KICK OR HIT CLOSE RANGE (USING ELBOWS, KNEES ETC).
A – Your best strategy against a kick boxer type opponent is to close – inside kicking range and clinch, – be aware of his knee and elbow attacks at this point – and take him down either using a body throw or a single leg pick up throw.

Q – AGAINST A GRAPPLER IS THE HIT AND POUND STRATEGY EFFECTIVE TO KNOCK OUT IF YOU LACK GROUND SKILLS AND WANT TO AVOID GOING TO GROUND.

A – In order to increase your chances of being able to counter a grappler, it is wise to know something about grappling or experience grappling. If you are unfamiliar with any sort of grappling you are likely to be taken down very quickly. I have seen where Boxers have beaten Grapplers and Grapplers have beaten Kickboxers, I've seen different strategies applied in these situations. So the best strategy for me against any opponent you know nothing about is to cross-Train and experience a multitude of attack as well as defence tactics. Cross training is special, a subject which I eluded on earlier. Distance is your main priority against a good grappler, and if you don't want to be taken down you should aim and learn to hit-and-pound hard and fast to knock out as soon as the grappler is in range.

Q – I AM PROFICIENT IN GROUNDFIGHTING IS IT WISE TO GO TO THE GROUND IN THE STREET OR SHOULD IT BE AVOIDED AS THERE IS A LARGE CHANCE OF INFLICTING INJURY TO MYSELF.

A – This is a two headed question. I would definitely avoid going to the ground in the street especially if you're fighting more than one person. There's a greater possibility of knee back neck or head injuries if it's a hard surface. There's a difference in taking a fall on the mat in the confines of a dojo and taking a fall on the hard surface on the street, so you must use certain practical street throws to avoid getting badly hurt.

Q – WHAT THROWS AND TAKEDOWNS WOULD YOU RECOMMEND IN TERMS OF EFFECTIVENESS AND SAFE FOR THE STREET ENVIRONMENT.

A – Sometimes the simplicity in your takedowns is the best method. Bruce Lee had various takedowns in his JKD Grappling arsenal, which were very much simple but street effective. Double leg or single leg takedown tackle, and single leg forward or backward trip or sweep which will have the opponent hit the ground first are good. I suggest you avoid going on your back with your opponent on top on the street. In JKD we are not always aiming for a lock or choke, once the opponent has been taken down we can continue to strike for a knock out to finish off. The options are there unlike some sports grappling arts.

Q – HOW DO I FIGHT A BIG GRAPPLER WHO HAS WEIGHT ADVANTAGE OVER ME.

A – I've seen smaller fighters beat big fighters, technique and strategy will be your best asset against a big grappler. Keep moving and if you end up in the clinch position tap into yourself the JKD philosophy of hitting first, hard and fast to the vulnerable areas which he'll be unsuspecting, or a pinch to a soft area to soften up his aggressiveness and control. If you end up on the ground, again striking in conjunction to grappling manoeuvres is an effective tactic against a big grappler to try to offset him.